Prose and Poetry from
the Old Testament

Crofts Classics

Prose and Poetry from the Old Testament

EDITED BY

James F. Fullington

Harlan Davidson, Inc.
Arlington Heights, Illinois 60004

Library of Congress Cataloging-in-Publication Data

Bible. O.T. English. Authorized. Selections. 1986.
   Prose and poetry from the Old Testament.

   (Crofts classics)
   Bibliography: p.
   I. Fullington, James F. (James Fitz-James)
II. Bible. O.T. English. Revised Standard.
Selections. 1986. III. Title.
[BS1091.F8   1986]   221.5′2036   86-4581
ISBN 0-88295-013-4 (pbk.)

Manufactured in the United States of America
90 89 88 87 MG 20 21 22 23

CONTENTS

INTRODUCTION

OF THE Old Testament books from which these selections have been taken, all but The Song of Songs and Proverbs are ultimately concerned with eternal problems of the human spirit—the nature of God, the nature of man, his purpose in life, his relation to God and to his fellow man. The time span of these writings is half a millennium, from the eighth to the third centuries before Christ. This period saw the Hebrew nation first standing at the peak of its wealth and power, then collapsing under the assaults of the great empires of Assyria and Babylonia, and finally settling down to the uneasy status of a vassal under Persians and Greeks. Yet it was during these centuries of national decline that the Jews developed one of the world's greatest religions, Judaism, out of which grew Christianity. The process began in the time of the prophets, between approximately 750 and 550 B.C.

Now although the prophets were mystics, in that they were possessed by a sense of the immanence of the Divine and of the directness of their communication with Him, they were also hard-headed realists, acute in their observation of contemporary social and political affairs and practical in their proposals. The problems which gave rise to their prophecies were real and immediate. Their people were engaged in an endless succession of devastating wars against powerful empires, wars which under the circumstances could have no outcome but national disaster. The nation was corroded by social evils—abysmal poverty, exploitation of the poor, corruption in high places, widespread perversion of justice, and the concentration of wealth and luxury in the hands of the few. The national religion, which should have been the guiding social force, refused to face the evils, much less try to ameliorate them. Priests and people were corrupted by alien religious cults; they accepted a practical polytheism, devoid of spiritual vitality and lacking in moral insight. The essence of the popular religion was an empty formalism, an almost exclusive concern with ritual and ceremony. It fostered complacency in the rich and afforded neither comfort nor hope to the miserable poor.

To the prophets, the impending disaster was the inevitable effect of these evils, which violated God's law as they perceived it. The core of their teaching was concisely expressed several centuries later: "What commandment is the first of all? Hear, O Israel, the Lord our God, the Lord is one; and thou shalt love the Lord thy God with all thy heart, and with all thy soul, and with all thy mind, and with all thy strength. The second is this, Thou shalt love thy neighbor as thyself." But these concepts were new when the prophets gave them expression. God is the sole omnipotent creator and director of the universe. Just and merciful Himself, He requires justice and mercy from His children. He abhors evil and punishes it, not for the sake of vengeance, but to bring about man's moral and spiritual regeneration. He rewards the good and comforts the afflicted. But "good" in God's eyes is not the performance of religious rites and ceremonies. "Good" is purity of heart, love of God and faith in Him, and justice and mercy to one's fellows. Out of the teaching of the prophets arose the first enduring ethical religion in the world.

The predictions of disaster by the earlier prophets expressed their clear insight into the inflexible course of events. Yet this was modified by the passionate conviction that God would not bring about the utter destruction of His chosen people. Hence, from Isaiah and Micah on, they promise that after a period of affliction and suffering, there will arise a purified Israel, dedicated to Jehovah and His law. Under the leadership of a prince who will be God's earthly vicar, Israel will "rebuild the nation," teach God's law to the Gentiles and so bring about a reign of universal peace and piety.

Regarded historically, the prophets were simply and immediately concerned with "old, unhappy, far-off things, and battles long ago." But they probed so deeply and with such clear insight into moral and religious problems that their words have a universal application. During 2500 years their poems have been a source of comfort and strength to the simple and the wise. For not only were they poets of great beauty and power, but they struggled with the most intimate problems of life and the human soul.

After the Exile, the prophetic fire burned out in Israel. The great literary contributions were now made by "wise men" or sages, practical philosophers who looked for inspiration to Wisdom. *Wisdom,* though sometimes regarded as a personified divine principle, generally referred to the worldly, practical, common sense which contributes to a happy and prosperous life. The sages were teachers, teachers of the young, expressing themselves in brief maxims or longer exhortations, by shrewd observations and warm personal appeals. The three wisdom books in the Hebrew Old Testament are Proverbs, Job, and Ecclesiastes. Proverbs is a compilation of earlier collections, completed probably in the third century, B.C. Many of the individual proverbs are very old. Their present form often may be due to the sages, who were authors as well as compilers. The tradition that Solomon composed some or all of Proverbs in unreliable.

The Book of Proverbs is entirely orthodox, in its assumption that the righteous and the wicked are rewarded as they deserve. With logical consistency, this doctrine had been given a corollary. Suffering and adversity is the result of sin; prosperity and happiness, of good. But the authors of Job and Ecclesiastes observed that the doctrine does not agree with the facts. About 400 B.C. the author of Job, who himself must have suffered and cried out a bitter "Why?" wrote his immortal poem on the problem of good and evil. Taking a folk tale about an ancient worthy named Job whose righteousness was rewarded after a period of severe affliction, he inserted in the midst of the action a series of dialogues between the suffering Job and his friends. Job is aware of his uprightness and his heartfelt fidelity to God—facts which God Himself privately admits—and agonizingly seeks an explanation for his suffering. His friends' answers play the variations on orthodox doctrine: Job must have sinned, possibly unwittingly; or, the punishment is inflicted for his good, for the purification of his soul; and, as Job's arguments continue, he is *ipso facto* a sinner. Job bitterly accuses God of injustice and demands that God give him a trial. Finally God replies with an answer that explains nothing. It is that God and His ways are past human comprehension. Nevertheless, Job is satisfied. He has had a vision of God and the assurance of His nearness and His concern.

Ecclesiastes deals with an even larger problem: What is the meaning and purpose of life? How can man obtain the greatest satisfaction from it. Although completely unorthodox, the book was included in the Old Testament because of its supposed Solomonic authorship. It comprises a number of loosely organized discourses made up of shrewd observations, reflections, and epigrammatic sayings. They represent the conclusions, not of a systematic philosopher, but, as we may suppose, an old man with wide experience and much common sense.

To Ecclesiastes the world is topsy-turvey, without discernible rhyme or reason. It is a world in which the best efforts may be defeated, virtue punished, vice rewarded, in short, where no cause and effect, no moral order can be perceived in human affairs. It is true that God determines everything on earth, but no man can discern His ways. The wise man will proceed cautiously, therefore, and observe the golden mean: "Be not righteous overmuch; be not overmuch wicked." The only satisfaction to be found is in life itself and in its simple pleasures. "There is nothing better for a man than that he should eat and drink and make his soul enjoy good in his labor."

Some time after the book's composition pious scribes, outraged by its unorthodoxy, tried to tone it down by inserting phrases or sentences to counter the more objectionable passages. These can often be recognised by even the lay reader, for they express ideas contrary to the current of Ecclesiastes' thought.

The Book of Psalms and The Song of Songs are collections of lyric poems. The former is a collection of 150 hymns for a wide range of occasions in public and private worship. A combination of several earlier collections dating back to the fifth century, it was not finally closed until the second century. A number of psalms are certainly older, possibly as old as David, who is credited by doubtful tradition with about half of them. Some of the authors were mere versifiers. Others were poets of great power, who have given us some of the world's finest religious song.

Despite traditional views, The Song of Songs appears to be neither religious allegory nor to have been composed by Solomon. It is probably best explained by certain oriental wedding ceremonies in which bride and groom play the parts of king and queen among their attendants and recite poetic speeches praising each other's beauty. It has been suggested that this poem, now in a fragmentary state, was written for some notable wedding, to be performed with music, chorus, and dance.

The King James translation is used in this volume for the books of the prophets and Psalms; the Revised Version is used for Job, Ecclesiastes, Proverbs, and the Song of Songs, where it is admittedly superior. (In the notes the Revised Version is referred to by the abbreviation, R.V.). In the attempt to print the greatest possible amount of material of literary merit in the limited space available, the editor has not felt bound to reproduce whole chapters or whole units from the original. The Old Testament is shot through with superfluous scribal interpolations, redundancies, matter which is irrelevant or meaningless to modern lay readers, and obscure passages which even Biblical scholars cannot agree in translating or interpreting. The editor makes no apology for excluding matter of this sort. He has made no other changes in the text. For the reader's convenience a Table of Chapter References is provided on page xiv.

In preparing this volume, the editor has utilized verse arrangements and other typographical features employed in *The Bible: Designed to be Read as Living Literature,* edited by E. S. Bates (Simon and Schuster) and *The Bible for Today,* edited by John Stirling (Oxford Press). Grateful acknowledgment is due the publishers for their permission to make this use of their publications.

Chronology

THE following list is offered with the caution that most of the dates indicated are approximate or subject to dispute. The dates assigned to the prophets do not indicate birth and death dates, but rather periods within which the prophet can be said to have flourished. All dates are B.C.

750.	Amos.
745-735.	Hosea.
738-700.	Isaiah.
740-700.	Micah.
722-721.	Fall of Samaria.
650-586.	Jeremiah.
587-586.	Fall of Jerusalem.
597-536.	The Exile.
593-571.	Ezekiel.

Late 6th century.   The "Unknown Prophet."
400 or earlier.   Job composed.
4th and 3rd centuries.   *Proverbs* collected.
3rd century.   *Song of Songs* composed.
     200.   *Ecclesiastes* composed.
2nd century.   Completion of the collection of *Psalms.*

TABLE OF CHAPTER REFERENCES

THE READER who wishes to refer from selections in this book to the corresponding text of an unabridged Bible may consult the following table. The left-hand entry indicates a page number in this book; the right-hand entry indicates the number of the Biblical chapter which begins on the page.

PROPHETICAL BOOKS

The Word of the Lord
That Came Unto
MICAH
THE MORASTHITE

IN THE DAYS OF JOTHAM, AHAZ, AND HEZEKIAH,
KINGS OF JUDAH, WHICH HE SAW CONCERNING
SAMARIA AND JERUSALEM.

"BUT IN THE LAST DAYS" [1]

But in the last days it shall come to pass,
That the mountain of the house of the Lord [2]
Shall be established in the top of the mountains,
And it shall be exalted above the hills;
And people shall flow unto it.

And many nations shall come, and say,
"Come, and let us go up to the mountain of the Lord,
And to the house of the God of Jacob;
And he will teach us of his ways,
And we will walk in his paths":
For the law shall go forth of Zion,
And the word of the Lord from Jerusalem.

[1] This is the first of several prophecies in this volume which
predict a day when the repentant and morally regenerated
Hebrew people, dedicated to Jehovah and his law, would
lead the world in a golden age of justice, universal peace,
and love of Jehovah   [2] **mountain of the house of the Lord** the
temple hill in Jerusalem

1

And he shall judge among many people,
And rebuke strong nations afar off;
And they shall beat their swords into plowshares,
And their spears into pruninghooks:
Nation shall not lift up a sword against nation,
Neither shall they learn war any more.
But they shall sit every man under his vine
And under his fig tree;
And none shall make them afraid:
For the mouth of the Lord of hosts hath spoken it.
For all people will walk every one in the name of his god,
And we will walk in the name of the Lord our God for ever
　　　and ever.

The Vision of
ISAIAH

❧

THE SON OF AMOZ, WHICH HE SAW CONCERNING
JUDAH AND JERUSALEM IN THE DAYS OF UZZIAH,
JOTHAM, AHAZ, AND HEZEKIAH, KINGS OF JUDAH.

"HEAR, O HEAVENS"

Hear, O heavens, and give ear, O earth:
For the Lord hath spoken:
"I have nourished and brought up children,
And they have rebelled against me.
The ox knoweth his owner,
And the ass his master's crib;
But Israel doth no know,
My people doth not consider."

Ah sinful nation, a people laden with iniquity,
A seed of evildoers, children that are corrupters!
They have forsaken the Lord,
They have provoked the Holy One of Israel unto anger,
They are gone away backward.

Why should ye be stricken any more? ye will revolt more
    and more;
The whole head is sick, and the whole heart faint.
From the sole of the foot even unto the head there is no
    soundness in it;
But wounds, and bruises, and putrifying sores:
They have not been closed, neither bound up, neither
    mollified with ointment.
Your country is desolate, your cities are burned with fire:
Your land. strangers devour it in your presence,

And it is desolate, as overthrown by strangers.
And the daughter of Zion is left as a cottage in a vineyard,
As a lodge in a garden of cucumbers, as a besieged city.
Except the Lord of hosts had left unto us a very small
    remnant,
We should have been as Sodom, we should have been like
    unto Gomorrah.

Hear the word of the Lord,
Ye rulers of Sodom!
Give ear unto the law of our God,
Ye people of Gomorrah!
"To what purpose is the multitude of your sacrifices unto
    me?"
Saith the Lord:
"I am full of the burnt offerings of rams,
And the fat of fed beasts;
And I delight not in the blood of bullocks,
Or of lambs, or of he-goats.
When ye come to appear before me,
Who hath required this at your hand,
To tread my courts?
Bring no more vain oblations;
Incense is an abomination unto me;
The new moons and sabbaths, the calling of assemblies,
I cannot away with;
It is iniquity, even the solemn meeting.
Your new moons and your appointed feasts my soul hateth:
They are a trouble unto me; I am weary to bear them.
And when ye spread forth your hands,
I will hide mine eyes from you:
Yea, when ye make many prayers,
I will not hear:
Your hands are full of blood.
Wash you, make you clean;
Put away the evil of your doings from before mine eyes;
Cease to do evil;
Learn to do well;
Seek judgment,[1] relieve the oppressed,
Judge the fatherless, plead for the widow.

judgment justice

Come now, and let us reason together,"
Saith the Lord:
"Though your sins be as scarlet,
They shall be as white as snow;
Though they be red like crimson,
They shall be as wool.
If ye be willing and obedient,
Ye shall eat the good of the land:
But if ye refuse and rebel,
Ye shall be devoured with the sword":
For the mouth of the Lord hath spoken it.

"BECAUSE THE DAUGHTERS OF ZION ARE HAUGHTY"

Because the daughters of Zion are haughty,
And walk with stretched forth necks and wanton eyes,
Walking and mincing as they go,
And making a tinkling with their feet:
Therefore the Lord will smite with a scab
The crown of the head of the daughters of Zion,
And the Lord will discover their secret parts.
In that day the Lord will take away
The bravery of their tinkling ornaments about their feet,
And their cauls, and their round tires like the moon,[2]
The chains, and the bracelets, and the mufflers,
The bonnets, and the ornaments of the legs,
And the headbands, and the tablets,[3] and the earrings,
The rings, and nose jewels,
The changeable suits of apparel,
And the mantles, and the wimples, and the crisping pins,
The glasses,[4] and the fine linen, and the hoods, and the veils.
And it shall come to pass,
That instead of sweet smell there shall be stink;
And instead of a girdle a rent;[5]
And instead of well-set hair baldness;
And instead of a stomacher a girding of sackcloth;
And burning instead of beauty.
Thy men shall fall by the sword,

[2] **tires** headdresses   [3] **tablets** R. V. perfume boxes   [4] **glasses**
mirrors   [5] **rent** R. V. rope, i.e., to bind the captive

And thy mighty in the war.
And her gates shall lament and mourn;
And she being desolate shall sit upon the ground.

And in that day seven women shall take hold of one man, saying, "We will eat our own bread, and wear our own apparel: only let us be called by thy name, to take away our reproach."

"AND THERE SHALL COME FORTH A ROD" [6]

And there shall come forth a rod out of the stem of Jesse,[7]
And a Branch shall grow out of his roots.
And the spirit of the Lord shall rest upon him,
The spirit of wisdom and understanding,
The spirit of counsel and might,
The spirit of knowledge and of the fear of the Lord;
And shall make him of quick understanding in the fear of
      the Lord:
And he shall not judge after the sight of his eyes,
Neither reprove after the hearing of his ears;
But with righteousness shall he judge the poor,
And reprove with equity for the meek of the earth;
And he shall smite the earth with the rod of his mouth,
And with the breath of his lips shall he slay the wicked.
And righteousness shall be the girdle of his loins,
And faithfulness the girdle of his reins.[8]
The wolf also shall dwell with the lamb,
And the leopard shall lie down with the kid;
And the calf and the young lion and the fatling together;
And a little child shall lead them.
And the cow and the bear shall feed;
Their young ones shall lie down together:
And the lion shall eat straw like the ox.
And the sucking child shall play on the hole of the asp,

[6] A prophecy of the Messianic (God's anointed) King, either already or soon to be born, who is to establish the reign of justice after Israel has been delivered from the oppressor. See note 1. [7] Jesse father of King David [8] reins kidneys, synonymous with *loins* in the preceding line. We would say *heart*.

And the weaned child shall put his hand on the cockatrice's
    den.
They shall not hurt nor destroy
In all my holy mountain:
For the earth shall be full of the knowledge of the Lord,
As the waters cover the sea.

"BEHOLD, I WILL STIR UP THE MEDES" [9]

Behold, I will stir up the Medes against them, which shall
not regard silver;

And as for gold, they shall not delight in it.
Their bows also shall dash the young men to pieces;
And they shall have no pity on the fruit of the womb;
Their eye shall not spare children.
And Babylon, the glory of kingdoms,
The beauty of the Chaldee's excellency,
Shall be as when God overthrew Sodom and Gomorrah.
It shall never be inhabited,
Neither shall it be dwelt in from generation to generation:
Neither shall the Arabian pitch tent there;
Neither shall the shepherds make their fold there.
But wild beasts of the desert shall lie there;
And their houses shall be full of doleful creatures;
And owls shall dwell there,
And satyrs shall dance there.
And the wild beasts of the islands shall cry in their desolate
    houses,
And dragons in their pleasant palaces:
And her time is near to come,
And her days shall not be prolonged.

For the Lord will have mercy on Jacob, and will yet
choose Israel, and set them in their own land: and the
strangers shall be joined with them, and they shall cleave
to the house of Jacob. And the people shall take them, and
bring them to their place: and the house of Israel shall
possess them in the land of the Lord for servants and hand-

[9] An oracle against Babylon

maids: and they shall take them captives, whose captives
they were; and they shall rule over their oppressors. And it
shall come to pass in the day that the Lord shall give thee
rest from thy sorrow, and from thy fear, and from the hard
bondage wherein thou wast made to serve, that thou shalt
take up this proverb against the king of Babylon, and say,

"How hath the oppressor ceased!
The golden city ceased!
The Lord hath broken the staff of the wicked,
And the sceptre of the rulers.
He who smote the people in wrath with a continual stroke,
He that ruled the nations in anger,
Is persecuted, and none hindereth.
The whole earth is at rest, and is quiet:
They break forth into singing.
Yea, the fir trees rejoice at thee,
And the cedars of Lebanon, saying,
'Since thou art laid down,
No feller is come up against us.'
Hell from beneath is moved for thee
To meet thee at thy coming:
It stirreth up the dead for thee,
Even all the chief ones of the earth;
It hath raised up from their thrones all the kings of the
    nations.
All they shall speak and say unto thee,
'Art thou also become weak as we?
Art thou become like unto us?'
Thy pomp is brought down to the grave,
And the noise of thy viols:
The worm is spread under thee,
And the worms cover thee.
How art thou fallen from heaven,
O Lucifer, son of the morning!
How art thou cut down to the ground,
Which didst weaken the nations!
For thou hast said in thine heart, 'I will ascend into heaven,
I will exalt my throne above the stars of God:
I will sit also upon the mount of the congregation,
In the sides of the north:

I will ascend above the heights of the clouds;
I will be like the most High.'
Yet thou shalt be brought down to hell,
To the sides of the pit.[10]
They that see thee shall narrowly look upon thee,
And consider thee, saying,
'Is this the man that made the earth to tremble,
That did shake kingdoms;
That made the world as a wilderness, and destroyed the
    cities thereof;
That opened not the house of his prisoners?'
All the kings of the nations, even all of them, lie in glory,
Every one in his own house.[11]
But thou art cast out of thy grave
Like an abominable branch,
And as the raiment of those that are slain,
Thrust through with a sword,
That go down to the stones of the pit;
As a carcase trodden under feet.'

"O LORD, THOU ART MY GOD"

O Lord, thou art my God; I will exalt thee;
I will praise thy name;
For thou hast done wonderful things;
Thy counsels of old are faithfulness and truth.
For thou hast made of a city a heap;
Of a defenced [12] city a ruin:
A palace of strangers to be no city;
It shall never be built.
Therefore shall the strong people glorify thee,
The city of the terrible nations shall fear thee.
For thou hast been a strength to the poor,
A strength to the needy in his distress,
A refuge from the storm,
A shadow from the heat,
When the blast of the terrible ones
Is as a storm against the wall.[13]

[10] **sides** R. V. uttermost parts   [11] **house** i.e. sepulchre   [12] **defenced** fortified   [13] meaning obscure

Thou shalt bring down the noise of strangers,
As the heat in a dry place;
Even the heat with the shadow of a cloud:
The branch of the terrible ones shall be brought low.

Lo, this is our God;
We have waited for him,
And he will save us:
This is the Lord;
We have waited for him,
We will be glad and rejoice in his salvation.

THE CHARACTER OF THE LIBERAL

Behold, a king shall reign in righteousness, and princes shall rule in judgment. And a man shall be as a hiding place from the wind, and a covert from the tempest; as rivers of water in a dry place, as the shadow of a great rock in a weary land. And the eyes of them that see shall not be dim, and the ears of them that hear shall hearken. The heart also of the rash shall understand knowledge, and the tongue of the stammerers shall be ready to speak plainly. The vile person shall be no more called liberal, nor the churl said to be bountiful. For the vile person will speak villainy, and his heart will work iniquity, to practise hypocrisy, and to utter error against the Lord, to make empty the soul of the hungry, and he will cause the drink of the thirsty to fail. The instruments also of the churl are evil: he deviseth wicked devices to destroy the poor with lying words, even when the needy speaketh right. But the liberal deviseth liberal things; and by liberal things shall he stand.

The Words of
JEREMIAH

THE SON OF HILKIAH, OF THE PRIESTS THAT WERE IN
ANATHOTH IN THE LAND OF BENJAMIN: TO WHOM
THE WORD OF THE LORD CAME IN THE DAYS OF
JOSIAH THE SON OF AMON KING OF JUDAH, IN THE
THIRTEENTH YEAR OF HIS REIGN. IT CAME ALSO IN
THE DAYS OF JEHOIAKIM THE SON OF JOSIAH KING
OF JUDAH, UNTO THE END OF THE ELEVENTH YEAR
OF ZEDEKIAH THE SON OF JOSIAH KING OF JUDAH,
UNTO THE CARRYING AWAY OF JERUSALEM CAPTIVE
IN THE FIFTH MONTH.

THE CALL OF JEREMIAH

THE word of the Lord came unto me, saying, "Before I
formed thee in the belly I knew thee; and before thou cam-
est forth out of the womb I sanctified thee, and I ordained
thee a prophet unto the nations."

Then said I, "Ah, Lord God! behold, I cannot speak; for
I am a child."

But the Lord said unto me, "Say not, 'I am a child': for
thou shalt go to all that I shall send thee, and whatsoever I
command thee thou shalt speak. Be not afraid [1] of their
faces: for I am with thee to deliver thee," saith the Lord.

Then the Lord put forth his hand, and touched my
mouth. And the Lord said unto me, "Behold, I have put
my words in thy mouth. See, I have this day set thee over

[1] **Be not afraid . . .** The prophets were opposed by many powerful people. Jeremiah was imprisoned and his life threat-
ened more than once.

11

the nations and over the kingdoms, to root out, and to pull down, and to destroy, and to throw down, to build, and to plant."

"TO WHOM SHALL I SPEAK AND GIVE WARNING?"

To whom shall I speak, and give warning, that they may hear?
Behold, their ear is uncircumcised,[2] and they cannot hearken:
Behold, the word of the Lord is unto them a reproach;
They have no delight in it.
Therefore I am full of the fury of the Lord;
I am weary with holding in:
I will pour it out upon the children abroad,
And upon the assembly of young men together:
For even the husband with the wife shall be taken,
The aged with him that is full of days.
And their houses shall be turned unto others,
With their fields and wives together:
"For I will stretch out my hand
Upon the inhabitants of the land," saith the Lord.
"For the least of them even unto the greatest of them
Every one is given to covetousness;
And from the prophet even unto the priest every one dealeth falsely.
They have healed also the hurt of the daughter of my people slightly,[3]
Saying, 'Peace, peace'; when there is no peace.

Were they ashamed when they had committed abomination?
Nay, they were not at all ashamed,
Neither could they blush:
Therefore they shall fall among them that fall:
At the time that I visit them they shall be cast down," saith the Lord.

Thus saith the Lord,
"Stand ye in the ways, and see,

[2] **uncircumcised** i.e., unsanctified [3] **They have healed . . .** (treated) the wound only superficially

And ask for the old paths, where is the good way,
And walk therein, and ye shall find rest for your souls.
But they said, 'We will not walk therein.'
Also I set watchmen [4] over you, saying,
'Hearken to the sound of the trumpet.'
But they said, 'We will not hearken.'

Therefore hear, ye nations,
And know, O congregation, what is among them.
Hear, O earth:
Behold, I will bring evil upon this people,
Even the fruit of their thoughts,
Because they have not hearkened unto my words,
Nor to my law, but rejected it.
To what purpose cometh there to me incense from Sheba,
And the sweet cane [5] from a far country?
Your burnt offerings are not acceptable,
Nor your sacrifices sweet unto me."

Therefore thus saith the Lord,
"Behold, I will lay stumblingblocks before this people,
And the fathers and the sons together shall fall upon them;
The neighbour and his friend shall perish."

"THE WAY OF THE HEATHEN"

"Learn not the way of the heathen,
And be not dismayed at the signs of heaven; [6]
For the heathen are dismayed at them.
For the customs of the people are vain:
For one cutteth a tree out of the forest,
The work of the hands of the workman, with the ax.
They deck it with silver and with gold;
They fasten it with nails and with hammers, that it move
    not.
They are upright as the palm tree, but speak not:
They must needs be borne, because they cannot go.

[4] **watchmen** the prophets [5] **sweet cane** from which incense
was made [6] **signs of heaven** celestial phenomena, as move-
ments of the planets, eclipses, comets, all of which figured
prominently in Babylonian religious cults

Be not afraid of them;
For they cannot do evil,
Neither also is it in them to do good."

But they are altogether brutish and foolish:
The stock [7] is a doctrine of vanities.
Silver spread into plates is brought from Tarshish,
And gold from Uphaz,
The work of the workman, and of the hands of the founder: [8]
Blue and purple is their clothing:
They are all the work of cunning men.

But the Lord is the true God,
He is the living God, and an everlasting king:
At his wrath the earth shall tremble,
And the nations shall not be able to abide his indignation.
He hath made the earth by his power,
He hath established the world by his wisdom,
And hath stretched out the heavens by his discretion.
When he uttereth his voice, there is a multitude of waters
    in the heavens,
And he causeth the vapours to ascend from the ends of the
    earth;
He maketh lightnings with rain,
And bringeth forth the wind out of his treasures. [9]
Every man is brutish in his knowledge:
Every founder is confounded by the graven image:
For his molten image is falsehood,
And there is no breath in them.
They are vanity, and the work of errors:
In the time of their visitation they shall perish.

The portion [10] of Jacob is not like them:
For he is the former of all things;
And Israel is the rod [11] of his inheritance:
The Lord of hosts is his name.

[7] **stock** stick, wood, i.e., the idol   [8] **founder** R. V. goldsmith
[9] **treasures** R. V. treasuries. Storms were thought of as being
kept by God in store houses.   [10] **portion** inheritance. The
phrase refers to Jehovah.   [11] **rod** R. V. tribe

PARABLE OF THE POTTER

The word which came to Jeremiah from the Lord, saying, "Arise, and go down to the potter's house, and there I will cause thee to hear my words."

Then I went down to the potter's house, and, behold, he wrought a work on the wheels. And the vessel that he made of clay was marred in the hand of the potter: so he made it again another vessel, as seemed good to the potter to make it.

Then the word of the Lord came to me, saying, "O house of Israel, cannot I do with you as this potter?" saith the Lord. "Behold, as the clay is in the potter's hand, so are ye in my hand, O house of Israel. At what instant I shall speak concerning a nation, and concerning a kingdom, to pluck up, and to pull down, and to destroy it; if that nation, against whom I have pronounced, turn from their evil, I will repent of the evil that I thought to do unto them. And at what instant I shall speak concerning a nation, and concerning a kingdom, to build and to plant it; if it do evil in my sight, that it obey not my voice, then I will repent of the good wherewith I said I would benefit them."

"O LORD, THOU HAST DECEIVED ME"

O Lord, thou hast deceived me, and I was deceived:
Thou art stronger than I, and hast prevailed:
I am in derision daily, every one mocketh me.
For since I spoke, I cried out,
I cried violence and spoil;
Because the word of the Lord was made a reproach unto me,
And a derision, daily.
Then I said, "I will not make mention of him,
Nor speak any more his name."

But his word was in mine heart as a burning fire shut up in
    my bones,
And I was weary with forbearing,
And I could not stay.
For I heard the defaming of many,
Fear on every side.

"Report," [12] say they,
"And we will report it."
All my familiars watched for my halting,
Saying, "Peradventure he will be enticed, and we shall pre-
     vail against him,
And we shall take our revenge on him."
But the Lord is with me as a mighty terrible one:
Therefore my persecutors shall stumble, and they shall not
     prevail:
They shall be greatly ashamed;
For they shall not prosper:
Their everlasting confusion shall never be forgotten.
But, O Lord of hosts, that triest the righteous,
And seest the reins and the heart,
Let me see thy vengeance on them:
For unto thee have I opened my cause.

Cursed be the day wherein I was born:
Let not the day wherein my mother bore me be blessed.
Cursed be the man who brought tidings to my father,
Saying, "A man child is born unto thee";
Making him very glad.
And let that man be as the cities which the Lord overthrew,
     and repented not:
And let him hear the cry in the morning, and the shouting
     at noontide;
Because he slew me not from the womb;
Or that my mother might have been my grave,
And her womb to be always great with me.
Wherefore came I forth out of the womb to see labour and
     sorrow,
That my days should be consumed with shame?

[12] **report** R. V. denounce

The Book of the Prophet
EZEKIEL

THE VISION OF GOD

Now it came to pass in the thirtieth year, in the fourth month, in the fifth day of the month, as I was among the captives by the river of Chebar, that the heavens were opened, and I saw visions of God.

And I looked, and, behold, a whirlwind came out of the north, a great cloud, and a fire infolding itself, and a brightness was about it, and out of the midst thereof as the colour of amber, out of the midst of the fire. Also out of the midst thereof came the likeness of four living creatures.[1] And this was their appearance; they had the likeness of a man. And every one had four faces, and every one had four wings. And their feet were straight feet; and the sole of their feet was like the sole of a calf's foot: and they sparkled like the colour of burnished brass. And they had the hands of a man under their wings on their four sides; and they four had their faces and their wings. Their wings were joined one to another; they turned not when they went; they went every one straight forward. As for the likeness of their faces, they four had the face of a man, and the face of a lion, on the right side: and they four had the face of an ox on the left side; they four also had the face of an eagle. Thus were their faces: and their wings were stretched upward; two wings of every one were joined one to another, and two covered their bodies. And they went every one straight forward: whither the spirit[2] was to go, they went; and they turned not when they went. As for the likeness of the living creatures, their appearance was like burning

[1] **creatures** Elsewhere Ezekiel calls them *cherubim.* The reader should go to the commentaries for attempts to interpret and harmonize the details of the vision.   [2] **spirit** the spirit of God

coals of fire, and like the appearance of lamps; it went up and down among the living creatures; and the fire was bright, and out of the fire went forth lightning. And the living creatures ran and returned as the appearance of a flash of lightning.

Now as I beheld the living creatures, behold one wheel upon the earth by the living creatures, with his four faces. The appearance of the wheels and their work was like unto the colour of a beryl: and they four had one likeness: and their appearance and their work was as it were a wheel in the middle of a wheel. When they went, they went upon their four sides: and they turned not when they went. As for their rings,[3] they were so high that they were dreadful; and their rings were full of eyes round about them four. And when the living creatures went, the wheels went by[4] them: and when the living creatures were lifted up from the earth, the wheels were lifted up. Whithersoever the spirit was to go, they went, thither was their spirit to go; and the wheels were lifted up over against them: for the spirit of the living creature was in the wheels. When those went, these went; and when those stood, these stood; and when those were lifted up from the earth, the wheels were lifted up over against them: for the spirit of the living creature was in the wheels. And the likeness of the firmament upon the heads of the living creature was as the colour of the terrible crystal, stretched forth over their heads above. And under the firmament were their wings straight, the one toward the other: every one had two, which covered on this side, and every one had two, which covered on that side, their bodies. And when they went, I heard the noise of their wings, like the noise of great waters, as the voice of the Almighty, the voice of speech,[5] as the noise of a host: when they stood, they let down their wings. And there was a voice from the firmament that was over their heads, when they stood, and had let down their wings.

And above the firmament that was over their heads was the likeness of a throne, as the appearance of a sapphire stone: and upon the likeness of the throne was the likeness

[3] **rings** felloes   [4] **by** R. V. beside   [5] **voice of speech** R. V. noise of tumult

as the appearance of a man above upon it. And I saw as the colour of amber, as the appearance of fire round about within it, from the appearance of his loins even upward, and from the appearance of his loins even downward, I saw as it were the appearance of fire, and it had brightness round about. As the appearance of the bow that is in the cloud in the day of rain, so was the appearance of the brightness round about. This was the appearance of the likeness of the glory of the Lord.

THE LAMENTATION FOR TYRE [6]

The word of the Lord came again unto me, saying, "Now, thou Son of Man, take up a lamentation for Tyrus; and say unto Tyrus, 'O thou that are situate at the entry of the sea, which art a merchant of the people for many isles, thus saith the Lord God: "O Tyrus, thou hast said, 'I am of perfect beauty.' Thy borders are in the midst of the seas, thy builders have perfected thy beauty. They have made all thy ship boards of fir trees of Senir: they have taken cedars from Lebanon to make masts for thee. Of the oaks of Bashan have they made thine oars; the company of the Ashurites have made thy benches of ivory,[7] brought out of the isles of Chittim. Fine linen with broidered work from Egypt was that which thou spreadest forth to be thy sail; blue and purple from the isles of Elishah was that which covered thee. The inhabitants of Sidon and Arvad were thy mariners: thy wise men, O Tyrus, that were in thee, were thy pilots. The ancients of Gebal and the wise men thereof were in thee thy calkers: all the ships of the sea with their mariners were in thee to occupy thy merchandise. They of Persia and of Lud and of Phut were in thine army, thy men of war: they hanged the shield and helmet in thee; they set forth thy comeliness. The men of Arvad with thine army were upon thy walls round about, and the Gammadims were in thy towers: they hanged their shields upon thy walls

[6] **Tyre,** the greatest commercial city and maritime port in the ancient world. Ezekiel expected Nebuchadnezzar, the Babylonian, to overthrow the city; but his prophecy was unfulfilled.
[7] **benches of ivory** R. V. suggests, benches of boxwood inlaid with ivory

round about; they have made thy beauty perfect. Tarshish [8] was thy merchant by reason of the multitude of all kind of riches; with silver, iron, tin, and lead, they traded in thy fairs. Javan, Tubal, and Meshech, they were thy merchants: they traded the persons of men and vessels of brass in thy market. They of the house of Togarmah traded in thy fairs with horses and horsemen and mules. The men of Dedan were thy merchants; many isles were the merchandise of thine hand: they brought thee for a present horns of ivory and ebony. Syria was thy merchant by reason of the multitude of the wares of thy making: they occupied in thy fairs with emeralds, purple, and broidered work, and fine linen, and coral, and agate. Judah, and the land of Israel, they were thy merchants: they traded in thy market wheat of Minnith, and Pannag, and honey, and oil, and balm. Damascus was thy merchant in the multitude of the wares of thy making, for the multitude of all riches; in the wine of Helbon, and white wool. Dan also and Javan going to and fro occupied in thy fairs: bright iron, cassia, and calamus, were in thy market. Dedan was thy merchant in precious clothes for chariots. Arabia, and all the princes of Kedar, they occupied with thee in lambs, and rams, and goats: in these were they thy merchants. The merchants of Sheba and Raamah, they were thy merchants: they occupied in thy fairs with chief of all spices, and with all precious stones, and gold. Haran, and Canneh, and Eden, the merchants of Sheba, Asshur, and Chilmad, were thy merchants. These were thy merchants in all sorts of things, in blue clothes, and broidered work, and in chests of rich apparel, bound with cords, and made of cedar, among thy merchandise. The ships of Tarshish did sing of thee in thy market: and thou wast replenished, and made very glorious in the midst of the seas.

" ' "Thy rowers have brought thee into great waters: the east wind hath broken thee in the midst of the seas. Thy

---

[8] **Tarshish,** in southern Spain, "farthest west" to the ancients. Here begins a list of products brought to Tyre for trade. Among the more important of the unfamiliar place names, the following are identified: Javan, Tubal, Meshech = the Greeks of Asia Minor and the Aegean. Togarmah = Armenia. Dedan = Rhodes. Sheba is in south Arabia. Asshur = Assyria.

riches, and thy fairs, thy merchandise, thy mariners, and thy pilots, thy calkers; and the occupiers of thy merchandise, and all thy men of war, that are in thee, and in all thy company which is in the midst of thee, shall fall into the midst of the seas in the day of thy ruin. The suburbs shall shake at the sound of the cry of thy pilots. And all that handle the oar, the mariners, and all the pilots of the sea, shall come down from their ships, they shall stand upon the land; and shall cause their voice to be heard against thee, and shall cry bitterly, and shall cast up dust upon their heads, they shall wallow themselves in the ashes: and they shall make themselves utterly bald for thee, and gird them with sackcloth, and they shall weep for thee with bitterness of heart and bitter wailing. And in their wailing they shall take up a lamentation for thee, and lament over thee, saying, 'What city is like Tyrus, like the destroyed in the midst of the sea?' When thy wares went forth out of the seas, thou filledst many people; thou didst enrich the kings of the earth with the multitude of thy riches and of thy merchandise. In the time when thou shalt be broken by the seas in the depths of the waters thy merchandise and all thy company in the midst of thee shall fall. All the inhabitants of the isles shall be astonished at thee, and their kings shall be sore afraid, they shall be troubled in their countenance. The merchants among the people shall hiss at thee; thou shalt be a terror, and never shalt be any more." ' "

THE VALLEY OF DRY BONES [9]

The hand of the Lord was upon me, and carried me out in the spirit of the Lord, and set me down in the midst of the valley which was full of bones, and caused me to pass by them round about: and, behold, there were very many in the open valley; and, lo, they were very dry.

And he said unto me, "Son of Man, can these bones live?" And I answered, "O Lord God, thou knowest."

Again he said unto me, "Prophesy upon these bones, and say unto them, 'O ye dry bones, hear the word of the Lord. Thus saith the Lord God unto these bones: "Behold, I will

[9] A vision of the resurrection of the Jewish nation, which has come to have a more general implication

cause breath to enter into you, and ye shall live: and I will lay sinews upon you, and will bring up flesh upon you, and cover you with skin, and put breath in you, and ye shall live; and ye shall know that I am the Lord." ' "

So I prophesied as I was commanded: and as I prophesied, there was a noise, and behold a shaking, and the bones came together, bone to his bone. And when I beheld, lo, the sinews and the flesh came up upon them, and the skin covered them above: but there was no breath in them.

Then he said unto me, "Prophesy unto the wind, prophesy, Son of Man, and say to the wind, 'Thus saith the Lord God: "Come from the four winds, O breath, and breathe upon these slain, that they may live." ' "

So I prophesied as he commanded me, and the breath came into them, and they lived, and stood up upon their feet, an exceeding great army.

Then he said unto me, "Son of Man, these bones are the whole house of Israel: behold, they say, 'Our bones are dried, and our hope is lost: we are cut off for our parts.' Therefore prophesy and say unto them, 'Thus saith the Lord God: "Behold, O my people, I will open your graves, and cause you to come up out of your graves, and bring you into the land of Israel. And ye shall know that I am the Lord, when I have opened your graves, O my people, and brought you up out of your graves, and shall put my spirit in you, and ye shall live, and I shall place you in your own land: then shall ye know that I the Lord have spoken it, and performed it," saith the Lord.' "

THE UNKNOWN PROPHET
of The Exile[1]

"Comfort ye, comfort ye my people,"
Saith your God.
"Speak ye comfortably to Jerusalem,
And cry unto her,
That her warfare is accomplished,
That her iniquity is pardoned:
For she hath received of the Lord's hand
Double for all her sins."

The voice of him that crieth in the wilderness,
"Prepare ye the way of the Lord,
Make straight in the desert a highway for our God.
Every valley shall be exalted,
And every mountain and hill shall be made low:
And the crooked shall be made straight,
And the rough places plain:
And the glory of the Lord shall be revealed,
And all flesh shall see it together:
For the mouth of the Lord hath spoken it."

The voice said, "Cry."
And he said, "What shall I cry?"
"All flesh is grass,
And all the goodliness thereof is as the flower of the field:
The grass withereth, the flower fadeth:
Because the spirit of the Lord bloweth upon it:

[1] Chaps. 40-55 of the Book of Isaiah contain oracles of an unknown prophet, sometimes called Deutero-Isaiah or the Second Isaiah. He was a contemporary of Ezekiel and like him lived among the exiles in Babylonia.

23

Surely the people is grass.
The grass withereth, the flower fadeth:
But the word of our God shall stand for ever.

O Zion, that bringest good tidings,[2]
Get thee up into the high mountain;
O Jerusalem, that bringest good tidings,
Lift up thy voice with strength;
Lift it up,
Be not afraid;
Say unto the cities of Judah,
"Behold your God!"

Behold, the Lord God will come with strong hand,
And his arm shall rule for him:
Behold, his reward is with him,
And his work before him.
He shall feed his flock like a shepherd:
He shall gather the lambs with his arm,
And carry them in his bosom,
And shall gently lead those that are with young.

Who hath measured the waters in the hollow of his hand,
And meted out heaven with the span,
And comprehended the dust of the earth in a measure,
And weighed the mountains in scales,
And the hills in a balance?

Who hath directed the Spirit of the Lord,
Or being his counsellor hath taught him?
With whom took he counsel,
And who instructed him,
And taught him in the path of judgment,
And taught him knowledge,
And showed to him the way of understanding?

Behold, the nations are as a drop of a bucket,
And are counted as the small dust of the balance:
Behold, he taketh up the isles as a very little thing.

[2] R. V.: "O thou that bringest good tidings to Zion." Similarly with the second line following.

And Lebanon is not sufficient to burn,
Nor the beasts thereof sufficient for a burnt offering.
All nations before him are as nothing;
And they are counted to him less than nothing, and vanity.

To whom then will ye liken God?
Or what likeness will ye compare unto him?
Have ye not known? have ye not heard?
Hath it not been told you from the beginning?
Have ye not understood from the foundations of the earth?
It is he that sitteth upon the circle of the earth,
And the inhabitants thereof are as grasshoppers;
That stretcheth out the heavens as a curtain,
And spreadeth them out as a tent to dwell in;
That bringeth the princes to nothing;
He maketh the judges of the earth as vanity.
Yea, they shall not be planted;
Yea, they shall not be sown;
Yea, their stock shall not take root in the earth;
And he shall also blow upon them, and they shall wither,
And the whirlwind shall take them away as stubble.

"To whom then will ye liken me,
Or shall I be equal?" saith the Holy One.
Lift up your eyes on high,
And behold who hath created these things,
That bringeth out their host by number:
He calleth them all by names
By the greatness of his might, for that he is strong in power;
Not one faileth.

Why sayest thou, O Jacob,
And speakest, O Israel,
"My way is hid from the Lord,
And my judgment is passed over from my God?"
Hast thou not known?
Hast thou not heard,
That the everlasting God,
The Lord, the Creator of the ends of the earth,
Fainteth not, neither is weary?
There is no searching of his understanding.

He giveth power to the faint;
And to them that have no might he increaseth strength.
Even the youths shall faint and be weary,
And the young men shall utterly fall:
But they that wait upon the Lord shall renew their strength;
They shall mount up with wings as eagles;
They shall run, and not be weary;
And they shall walk, and not faint.

"BEHOLD, MY SERVANT SHALL DEAL PRUDENTLY" [3]

Behold, my servant shall deal prudently,
He shall be exalted and extolled, and be very high.
As many were astonished at thee;
His visage was so marred more than any man,
And his form more than the sons of men:
So shall he sprinkle many nations; [4]
The kings shall shut their mouths at him:
For that which had not been told them shall they see;
And that which they had not heard shall they consider.

Who hath believed our report?
And to whom is the arm of the Lord revealed?
For he shall grow up before him as a tender plant,
And as a root out of a dry ground:
He hath no form nor comeliness;
And when we shall see him, there is no beauty that we
    should desire him.
He is despised and rejected of men;
A man of sorrows, and acquainted with grief:
And we hid as it were our faces from him;
He was despised, and we esteemed him not.

Surely he hath borne our griefs,
And carried our sorrows:
Yet we did esteem him stricken,

[3] This is one of several "Servant Songs" by this author. Orthodox Judaism has always seen the Servant as the Jewish nation,
suffering to redeem the sins of the world. Orthodox Christianity
is based upon the assumption that he is Jesus Christ.   [4] The
verse is obscure

Smitten of God, and afflicted.
But he was wounded for our transgressions,
He was bruised for our iniquities:
The chastisement of our peace was upon him; [5]
And with his stripes we are healed.
All we like sheep have gone astray;
We have turned every one to his own way;
And the Lord hath laid on him
The iniquity of us all.

He was oppressed, and he was afflicted,
Yet he opened not his mouth:
He is brought as a lamb to the slaughter,
And as a sheep before her shearers is dumb,
So he openeth not his mouth.
He was taken from prison and from judgment:
And who shall declare his generation? [6]
For he was cut off out of the land of the living:
For the transgression of my people was he stricken.
And he made his grave with the wicked,
And with the rich in his death;
Because he had done no violence,
Neither was any deceit in his mouth.

Yet it pleased the Lord to bruise him;
He hath put him to grief:
When thou shalt make his soul an offering for sin,
The pleasure of the Lord shall prosper in his hand. [7]
He shall see of the travail of his soul, and shall be satisfied:
By his knowledge shall my righteous servant justify many;
For he shall bear their iniquities.
Therefore will I divide him a portion with the great,
And he shall divide the spoil with the strong;
Because he hath poured out his soul unto death:
And he was numbered with the transgressors;
And he bore the sin of many,
And made intercession for the transgressors.

[5] The essential meaning appears in the preceding line   [6] Meaning obscure   [7] Meaning obscure

"FOR A SMALL MOMENT HAVE I FORSAKEN THEE"

"For a small moment have I forsaken thee;
But with great mercies will I gather thee.
In a little wrath I hid my face from thee for a moment;
But with everlasting kindness will I have mercy on thee,"
Saith the Lord thy Redeemer.
"For this is as the waters of Noah unto me:
For as I have sworn that the waters of Noah should no more
    go over the earth;
So have I sworn that I would not be wroth with thee, nor
    rebuke thee.
For the mountains shall depart,
And the hills be removed;
But my kindness shall not depart from thee,
Neither shall the covenant of my peace be removed,"
Saith the Lord that hath mercy on thee.

"O thou afflicted,
Tossed with tempest, and not comforted,
Behold, I will lay thy stones with fair colours,
And lay thy foundations with sapphires.
And I will make thy windows of agates,
And thy gates of carbuncles,
And all thy borders of pleasant stones.
And all thy children shall be taught of the Lord;
And great shall be the peace of thy children."

"HO, EVERY ONE THAT THIRSTETH"

"Ho, every one that thirsteth, come ye to the waters,
And he that hath no money; come ye, buy, and eat;
Yea, come, buy wine and milk
Without money and without price.
Wherefore do ye spend money for that which is not bread?
And your labour for that which satisfieth not?
Hearken diligently unto me, and eat ye that which is good,
And let your soul delight itself in fatness.

Seek ye the Lord while he may be found,
Call ye upon him while he is near:

Let the wicked forsake his way,
And the unrighteous man his thoughts:
And let him return unto the Lord,
And he will have mercy upon him;
And to our God,
For he will abundantly pardon.
For my thoughts are not your thoughts,
Neither are your ways my ways," saith the Lord.
"For as the heavens
Are higher than the earth,
So are my ways higher than your ways,
And my thoughts than your thoughts.
For as the rain cometh down, and the snow from heaven,
And returneth not thither, but watereth the earth,
And maketh it bring forth and bud,
That it may give seed to the sower, and bread to the eater:
So shall my word be that goeth forth out of my mouth:
It shall not return unto me void,
But it shall accomplish that which I please,
And it shall prosper in the thing whereto I sent it.

For ye shall go out with joy,
And be led forth with peace:
The mountains and the hills shall break forth before you
        into singing,
And all the trees of the field shall clap their hands.
Instead of the thorn shall come up the fir tree,
And instead of the brier shall come up the myrtle tree:
And it shall be to the Lord for a name;
For an everlasting sign that shall not be cut off."

The Book of
PSALMS

Psalm One

Blessed is the man that walketh not in the counsel of the
    ungodly,
Nor standeth in the way of sinners,
Nor sitteth in the seat of the scornful.
But his delight is in the law of the Lord;
And in his law doth he meditate day and night.
And he shall be like a tree planted by the rivers of water,
That bringeth forth his fruit in his season;
His leaf also shall not wither;
And whatsoever he doeth shall prosper.
The ungodly are not so;
But are like the chaff which the wind driveth away.
Therefore the ungodly shall not stand in the judgment,
Nor sinners in the congregation of the righteous.
For the Lord knoweth the way of the righteous;
But the way of the ungodly shall perish.

Psalm Eight

O Lord our Lord,
How excellent is thy name in all the earth!
Who hast set thy glory above the heavens.
Out of the mouth of babes and sucklings hast thou ordained
    strength
Because of thine enemies,
That thou mightest still the enemy and the avenger.[1]
When I consider thy heavens, the work of thy fingers,
The moon and the stars, which thou hast ordained;
What is man, that thou art mindful of him?

[1] **avenger** revengeful

And the son of man, that thou visitest him?
For thou hast made him a little lower than the angels,
And hast crowned him with glory and honour.
Thou madest him to have dominion over the works of thy
    hands;
Thou hast put all things under his feet:
All sheep and oxen,
Yea, and the beasts of the field;
The fowl of the air, and the fish of the sea,
And whatsoever passeth through the paths of the seas.
O Lord our Lord,
How excellent is thy name in all the earth!

Psalm Fifteen

Lord, who shall abide in thy tabernacle?
Who shall dwell in thy holy hill? [2]
"He that walketh uprightly, and worketh righteousness,
And speaketh the truth in his heart.
He that backbiteth not with his tongue,
Nor doeth evil to his neighbour,
Nor taketh up a reproach against his neighbour.
In whose eyes a vile person is contemned;
But he honoureth them that fear the Lord.
He that sweareth to his own hurt, and changeth not.
He that putteth not out his money to usury,
Nor taketh reward against the innocent.
He that doeth these things shall never be moved."

Psalm Nineteen

The heavens declare the glory of God;
And the firmament showeth his handiwork.
Day unto day uttereth speech, [3]

[2] **holy hill** The Jerusalem temple was built on a hill. Hence,
hill, mountain, and similar metaphors are used for the temple.
[3] Dayly and nightly these things show or speak of God's glory
and power

And night unto night showeth knowledge.
There is no speech nor language,
Where their voice is not heard.
Their line is gone out through all the earth,
And their words to the end of the world.
In them hath he set a tabernacle for the sun,
Which is as a bridegroom coming out of his chamber,
And rejoiceth as a strong man to run a race.
His going forth is from the end of the heaven,
And his circuit unto the ends of it:
And there is nothing hid from the heat thereof.
The law of the Lord is perfect, converting the soul:
The testimony of the Lord is sure, making wise the simple.
The statutes of the Lord are right, rejoicing the heart:
The commandment of the Lord is pure, enlightening the
    eyes.
The fear of the Lord is clean, enduring for ever:
The judgments of the Lord are true and righteous alto-
    gether.
More to be desired are they than gold, yea, than much fine
    gold;
Sweeter also than honey and the honeycomb.
Moreover by them is thy servant warned;
In keeping of them there is great reward.
Who can understand [4] his errors?
Cleanse thou me from secret faults.
Keep back thy servant also from presumptuous sins;
Let them not have dominion over me: then shall I be
    upright,
And I shall be innocent from the great transgression.
Let the words of my mouth, and the meditation of my heart,
    be acceptable in thy sight,
O Lord, my strength, and my redeemer.

[4] **understand** R. V. discern

Psalm Twenty-three

The Lord is my shepherd; I shall not want.
He maketh me to lie down in green pastures;
He leadeth me beside the still waters.
He restoreth my soul;
He leadeth me in the paths of righteousness for his name's
     sake.
Yea, though I walk through the valley of the shadow of
     death,
I will fear no evil: for thou art with me;
Thy rod and thy staff they comfort me.
Thou preparest a table before me in the presence of mine
     enemies:
Thou anointest my head with oil; my cup runneth over.
Surely goodness and mercy shall follow me all the days of
     my life,
And I will dwell in the house of the Lord for ever.

Psalm Twenty-four

The earth is the Lord's, and the fulness thereof;
The world, and they that dwell therein.
For he hath founded it upon the seas,
And established it upon the floods.
Who shall ascend into the hill of the Lord?
Or who shall stand in his holy place?
He that hath clean hands, and a pure heart;
Who hath not lifted up his soul unto vanity, nor sworn
     deceitfully.[5]
He shall receive the blessing from the Lord,
And righteousness from the God of his salvation.
This is the generation of them that seek him,
That seek thy face, O Jacob.
Lift up your heads, O ye gates;
And be ye lift up, ye everlasting doors;

[5] sworn deceitfully, uttered falsehood

And the King of glory shall come in.
Who is this King of glory?
The Lord strong and mighty,
The Lord mighty in battle.
Lift up your heads, O ye gates;
Even lift them up, ye everlasting doors;
And the King of glory shall come in.
Who is this King of glory?
The Lord of hosts,
He is the King of glory.

Psalm Forty-two

As the hart panteth after the water brooks,
So panteth my soul after thee, O God.
My soul thirsteth for God, for the living God:
When shall I come and appear before God?
My tears have been my meat day and night,
While they [6] continually say unto me, "Where is thy God?"
When I remember these things, I pour out my soul in me:
For I had gone [7] with the multitude, I went with them to
     the house of God,
With the voice of joy and praise, with a multitude that kept
     holy-day.
Why art thou cast down, O my soul?
And why art thou disquieted in me?
Hope thou in God: for I shall yet praise him
For the help of his countenance.
O my God, my soul is cast down within me:
Therefore will I remember thee from the land of Jordan,
And of the Hermonites, from the hill Mizar.
Deep calleth unto deep at the noise of thy waterspouts;
All thy waves and thy billows are gone over me.
Yet the Lord will command his lovingkindness in the
     daytime,
And in the night his song shall be with me,
And my prayer unto the God of my life.

[6] they, men   [7] For I had gone R. V. How I went

I will say unto God my rock, "Why hast thou forgotten me?
Why go I mourning because of the oppression of the
enemy?"
As with a sword in my bones, mine enemies reproach me,
While they say daily unto me, "Where is thy God?"
Why art thou cast down, O my soul?
And why art thou disquieted within me?
Hope thou in God: for I shall yet praise him,
Who is the health of my countenance, and my God.

Psalm Ninety

Lord, thou hast been our dwelling place
In all generations.
Before the mountains were brought forth,
Or ever thou hadst formed the earth and the world,
Even from everlasting to everlasting, thou art God.
Thou turnest man to destruction; [8]
And sayest, "Return, ye children of men."
For a thousand years in thy sight
Are but as yesterday when it is past,
And as a watch in the night.
Thou carriest them away as with a flood; they are as a sleep:
In the morning they are like grass which groweth up.
In the morning it flourisheth, and groweth up;
In the evening it is cut down, and withereth.
For we are consumed by thine anger,
And by thy wrath are we troubled.
Thou hast set our iniquities before thee,
Our secret sins in the light of thy countenance.
For all our days are passed away in thy wrath:
We spend our years as a tale that is told.
The days of our years are threescore years and ten;
And if by reason of strength they be fourscore years,
Yet is their strength [9] labour and sorrow;
For it is soon cut off, and we fly away.
Who knoweth the power of thine anger?
Even according to thy fear, so is thy wrath.

[8] destruction R. V. dust   [9] strength R. V. pride

So teach us to number our days,
That we may apply our hearts unto wisdom.
Return, O Lord, how long?
And let it repent thee concerning thy servants.
O satisfy us early with thy mercy;
That we may rejoice and be glad all our days.
Make us glad according to the days wherein thou hast
   afflicted us,
And the years wherein we have seen evil.
Let thy work appear unto thy servants,
And thy glory unto their children.
And let the beauty of the Lord our God be upon us:
And establish thou the work of our hands upon us;
Yea, the work of our hands establish thou it.

Psalm Ninety-one

He that dwelleth in the secret place of the most High
Shall abide under the shadow of the Almighty.
I will say of the Lord, "He is my refuge and my fortress;
My God, in him will I trust."
Surely he shall deliver thee from the snare of the fowler,
And from the noisome pestilence.
He shall cover thee with his feathers,
And under his wings shalt thou trust;
His truth shall be thy shield and buckler.
Thou shalt not be afraid for the terror by night;
Nor for the arrow that flieth by day;
Nor for the pestilence that walketh in darkness;
Nor for the destruction that wasteth at noonday.
A thousand shall fall at thy side,
And ten thousand at thy right hand;
But it shall not come nigh thee.
Only with thine eyes shalt thou behold
And see the reward of the wicked.
Because thou hast made the Lord, which is my refuge,
Even the most High, thy habitation;
There shall no evil befall thee,
Neither shall any plague come nigh thy dwelling.

For he shall give his angels charge over thee,
To keep thee in all thy ways.
They shall bear thee up in their hands,
Lest thou dash thy foot against a stone.
Thou shalt tread upon the lion and adder;
The young lion and the dragon shalt thou trample under
feet.
Because he hath set his love upon me, therefore will I
deliver him: [10]
I will set him on high, because he hath known my name.
He shall call upon me, and I will answer him;
I will be with him in trouble;
I will deliver him, and honour him.
With long life will I satisfy him,
And show him my salvation.

Psalm One Hundred

Make a joyful noise unto the Lord, all ye lands.
Serve the Lord with gladness:
Come before his presence with singing.
Know ye that the Lord he is God:
It is he that hath made us, and not we ourselves;
We are his people, and the sheep of his pasture.
Enter into his gates [11] with thanksgiving,
And into his courts with praise:
Be thankful unto him, and bless his name.
For the Lord is good; his mercy is everlasting;
And his truth endureth to all generations.

Psalm One Hundred Three

Bless the Lord, O my soul,
And all that is within me, bless his holy name.
Bless the Lord, O my soul,
And forget not all his benefits:

[10] God is the speaker   [11] gates, of the Temple

Who forgiveth all thine iniquities;
Who healeth all thy diseases;
Who redeemeth thy life from destruction;
Who crowneth thee with lovingkindness and tender
    mercies;
Who satisfieth thy mouth with good things;
So that thy youth is renewed like the eagle's.
The Lord executeth righteousness
And judgment for all that are oppressed.
He made known his ways unto Moses,
His acts unto the children of Israel.
The Lord is merciful and gracious,
Slow to anger, and plenteous in mercy.
He will not always chide,
Neither will he keep his anger for ever.
He hath not dealt with us after our sins,
Nor rewarded us according to our iniquities.
For as the heaven is high above the earth,
So great is his mercy toward them that fear him.
As far as the east is from the west,
So far hath he removed our transgressions from us.
Like as a father pitieth his children,
So the Lord pitieth them that fear him.
For he knoweth our frame;
He remembereth that we are dust.
As for man, his days are as grass;
As a flower of the field, so he flourisheth.
For the wind passeth over it, and it is gone;
And the place thereof shall know it no more.
But the mercy of the Lord is from everlasting to everlasting
    upon them that fear him,
And his righteousness unto children's children;
To such as keep his covenant,
And to those that remember his commandments to do them.
The Lord hath prepared his throne in the heavens;
And his kingdom ruleth over all.
Bless the Lord, ye his angels,
That excel in strength, that do his commandments,
Hearkening unto the voice of his word.
Bless ye the Lord, all ye his hosts;
Ye ministers of his, that do his pleasure.

Bless the Lord, all his works
In all places of his dominion:
Bless the Lord, O my soul.

Psalm One Hundred Four

Bless the Lord, O my soul.
O Lord my God, thou art very great;
Thou art clothed with honour and majesty.
Who coverest thyself with light as with a garment;
Who stretchest out the heavens like a curtain; [12]
Who layeth the beams of his chambers in the waters;
Who maketh the clouds his chariot;
Who walketh upon the wings of the wind; [13]
Who maketh his angels spirits,
His ministers a flaming fire;
Who laid the foundations of the earth,
That it should not be removed for ever.
Thou coveredst it with the deep as with a garment;
The waters stood above the mountains.
At thy rebuke they fled;
At the voice of thy thunder they hastened away.
They go up by the mountains, they go down by the valleys
Unto the place which thou hast founded for them.
Thou hast set a bound that they may not pass over,
That they turn not again to cover the earth.
He sendeth the springs into the valleys,
Which run among the hills.
They give drink to every beast of the field;
The wild asses quench their thirst.
By them shall the fowls of the heaven have their habitation,
Which sing among the branches.
He watereth the hills from his chambers:
The earth is satisfied with the fruit of thy works.
He causeth the grass to grow for the cattle,
And herb for the service of man:
That he may bring forth food out of the earth;

[12] **curtain** better, *tent*   [13] R. V. "Who maketh the winds his messengers,/His ministers, a flaming fire"

And wine that maketh glad the heart of man,
And oil to make his face to shine,
And bread which strengtheneth man's heart.
The trees of the Lord are full of sap,
The cedars of Lebanon, which he hath planted,
Where the birds make their nests;
As for the stork, the fir trees are her house.
The high hills are a refuge for the wild goats,
And the rocks for the conies.
He appointed the moon for seasons;
The sun knoweth his going down.
Thou makest darkness, and it is night,
Wherein all the beasts of the forest do creep forth.
The young lions roar after their prey,
And seek their meat from God.
The sun ariseth, they gather themselves together,
And lay them down in their dens.
Man goeth forth unto his work
And to his labour until the evening.
O Lord, how manifold are thy works!
In wisdom hast thou made them all;
The earth is full of thy riches.
So is this great and wide sea,
Wherein are things creeping innumerable,
Both small and great beasts.
There go the ships;
There is that leviathan, whom thou hast made to play
     therein.
These wait all upon thee,
That thou mayest give them their meat in due season.
That thou givest them they gather;
Thou openest thine hand, they are filled with good.
Thou hidest thy face, they are troubled;
Thou takest away their breath, they die,
And return to their dust.
Thou sendest forth thy spirit, they are created,
And thou renewest the face of the earth.
The glory of the Lord shall endure for ever;
The Lord shall rejoice in his works.
He looketh on the earth, and it trembleth;
He toucheth the hills, and they smoke.

I will sing unto the Lord as long as I live;
I will sing praise to my God while I have my being.
My meditation of him shall be sweet;
I will be glad in the Lord.
Let the sinners be consumed out of the earth,
And let the wicked be no more.
Bless thou the Lord, O my soul.
Praise ye the Lord.

Psalm One Hundred Twenty-one

I will lift up mine eyes unto the hills,
From whence cometh my help.[14]
My help cometh from the Lord,
Which made heaven and earth.
He will not suffer thy foot to be moved;
He that keepeth thee will not slumber.
Behold, he that keepeth Israel
Shall neither slumber nor sleep.
The Lord is thy keeper;
The Lord is thy shade upon thy right hand.
The sun shall not smite thee by day,
Nor the moon by night.
The Lord shall preserve thee from all evil;
He shall preserve thy soul.
The Lord shall preserve thy going out and thy coming in
From this time forth, and even for evermore.

Psalm One Hundred Twenty-eight

Blessed is every one that feareth the Lord,
That walketh in his ways.
For thou shalt eat the labour of thine hands;
Happy shalt thou be, and it shall be well with thee.
Thy wife shall be as a fruitful vine by the sides of thine
    house;

[14] R. V. makes this a question

Thy children like olive plants round about thy table.
Behold, that thus shall the man be blessed
That feareth the Lord.
The Lord shall bless thee out of Zion,
And thou shalt see the good of Jerusalem all the days of thy
    life.
Yea, thou shalt see thy children's children,
And peace upon Israel.

Psalm One Hundred Thirty

Out of the depths have I cried unto thee, O Lord.
Lord, hear my voice:
Let thine ears be attentive to the voice of my supplications.
If thou, Lord, shouldest mark iniquities,
O Lord, who shall stand?
But there is forgiveness with thee,
That thou mayest be feared.
I wait for the Lord, my soul doth wait,
And in his word do I hope.
My soul waiteth for the Lord
More than they that watch for the morning,
I say, more than they that watch for the morning.
Let Israel hope in the Lord,
For with the Lord there is mercy,
And with him is plenteous redemption.
And he shall redeem Israel
From all his iniquities.

Psalm One Hundred Thirty-seven

By the rivers of Babylon,
There we sat down, yea, we wept,
When we remembered Zion.
We hanged our harps
Upon the willows in the midst thereof.
For there they that carried us away captive required of us
    a song,

And they that wasted us required of us mirth, saying,
"Sing us one of the songs of Zion."
How shall we sing the Lord's song
In a strange land?
If I forget thee, O Jerusalem,
Let my right hand forget her cunning.
If I do not remember thee,
Let my tongue cleave to the roof of my mouth;
If I prefer not Jerusalem above my chief joy.
Remember, O Lord, the children of Edom in the day of
    Jerusalem; [15]
Who said, "Raze it, raze it, even to the foundation thereof."
O daughter of Babylon, who art to be destroyed;
Happy shall he be that rewardeth thee as thou hast served
    us.
Happy shall he be that taketh and dasheth thy little ones
    against the stones.

Psalm One Hundred Thirty-nine

O Lord, thou hast searched me, and known me.
Thou knowest my downsitting and mine uprising,
Thou understandest my thought afar off.
Thou compasseth [16] my path and my lying down,
And art acquainted with all my ways.
For there is not a word in my tongue,
But lo, O Lord, thou knowest it altogether.
Thou hast beset me behind and before,
And laid thine hand upon me.
Such knowledge is too wonderful for me;
It is high, I cannot attain unto it.
Whither shall I go from thy spirit?
Or whither shall I flee from thy presence?
If I ascend up into heaven, thou art there;
If I make my bed in hell, behold, thou art there.
If I take the wings of the morning,

[15] **day of Jerusalem** the day of its capture and destruction. The Edomites and Hebrews were bitter enemies. [16] **compasseth** R. V. searchest out

And dwell in the uttermost parts of the sea,
Even there shall thy hand lead me,
And thy right hand shall hold me.
If I say, "Surely the darkness shall cover me,"
Even the night shall be light about me;
Yea, the darkness hideth not from thee,
But the night shineth as the day:
The darkness and the light are both alike to thee.
For thou hast possessed my reins;
Thou hast covered me in my mother's womb.
I will praise thee; for I am fearfully and wonderfully made:
Marvellous are thy works;
And that my soul knoweth right well.
My substance was not hid from thee,
When I was made in secret,
And curiously wrought in the lowest parts of the earth.
Thine eyes did see my substance, yet being unperfect;
And in thy book all my members were written,
Which in continuance were fashioned,
When as yet there was none of them.
How precious also are thy thoughts unto me, O God!
How great is the sum of them!

Psalm One Hundred Forty-eight

Praise ye the Lord.
Praise ye the Lord from the heavens:
Praise him in the heights.
Praise ye him, all his angels:
Praise ye him, all his hosts.
Praise ye him, sun and moon:
Praise him, all ye stars of light.
Praise him, ye heavens of heavens,
And ye waters that be above the heavens.
Let them praise the name of the Lord:
For he commanded, and they were created.
He hath also established them for ever and ever;
He hath made a decree which shall not pass.[17]

[17] **pass** R. V. pass away

Praise the Lord from the earth,
Ye dragons, and all deeps,
Fire and hail, snow and vapours,
Stormy wind fulfilling his word,
Mountains and all hills,
Fruitful trees and all cedars,
Beasts and all cattle,
Creeping things and flying fowl,
Kings of the earth and all people,
Princes and all judges of the earth:
Both young men and maidens,
Old men and children,
Let them praise the name of the Lord;
For his name alone is excellent; [18]
His glory is above the earth and heaven.
He also exalteth the horn of his people,
The praise of all his saints;
Even of the children of Israel, a people near unto him.
Praise ye the Lord.

[18] **excellent** R. V. exalted

The Book of
PROVERBS

To know wisdom and instruction;
To discern the words of understanding;
To receive instruction in wise dealing,
In righteousness and judgment and equity;
To give subtilty to the simple,
To the young man knowledge and discretion:
That the wise man may hear, and increase in learning;
And that the man of understanding may attain unto sound
     counsels:
To understand a proverb, and a figure;
The words of the wise, and their dark sayings.

The fear of the Lord is the beginning of knowledge:
But the foolish despise wisdom and instruction.

"WITHHOLD NOT GOOD"

Withhold not good from them to whom it is due,
When it is in the power of thine hand to do it.
Say not unto thy neighbour, Go, and come again,
And to morrow I will give;
When thou hast it by thee.
Devise not evil against thy neighbour,
Seeing he dwelleth securely by thee.
Strive not with a man without cause,
If he have done thee no harm.
Envy thou not the oppressor,
And choose none of his ways.
For the froward is abomination to the Lord:
But his secret is with the righteous.
The curse of the Lord is in the house of the wicked:
But he blesseth the habitation of the just.

Surely he scorneth the scorners:
But he giveth grace unto the lowly.
The wise shall inherit glory:
But shame shall be the promotion of fools.

"GO TO THE ANT, THOU SLUGGARD"

Go to the ant, thou sluggard;
Consider her ways, and be wise:
Which having no chief,
Overseer, or ruler,
Provideth her meat in the summer,
And gathereth her food in the harvest.

How long wilt thou sleep, O sluggard?
When wilt thou arise out of thy sleep?
Yet a little sleep, a little slumber,
A little folding of the hands to sleep:
So shall thy poverty, come as a robber,
And thy want as an armed man.

"THERE BE SIX THINGS WHICH THE LORD HATETH"

There be six things which the Lord hateth;
Yea, seven which are an abomination unto him:
Haughty eyes, a lying tongue,
And hands that shed innocent blood;
A heart that deviseth wicked imaginations,
Feet that be swift in running to mischief;
A false witness that uttereth lies,
And he that soweth discord among brethren.

"AT THE WINDOW OF MY HOUSE"

At the window of my house
I looked forth through my lattice;
And I beheld among the simple ones,
I discerned among the youths,
A young man void of understanding,
Passing through the street near her corner,
And he went the way to her house;

In the twilight, in the evening of the day,
In the blackness of night and the darkness.

And, behold, there met him a woman
With the attire of a harlot, and wily of heart.
She is clamorous and wilful;
Her feet abide not in her house:
Now she is in the streets, now in the broad places,
And lieth in wait at every corner.
So she caught him, and kissed him,
And with an impudent face she said unto him:

"Sacrifices of peace offerings are with me; [1]
This day have I paid my vows.
Therefore came I forth to meet thee,
Diligently to seek thy face, and I have found thee.
I have spread my couch with carpets of tapestry,
With striped cloths of the yarn of Egypt.
I have perfumed my bed
With myrrh, aloes, and cinnamon.
Come, let us take our fill of love until the morning;
Let us solace ourselves with loves.
For the goodman is not at home,
He is gone a long journey:
He hath taken a bag of money with him;
He will come home at the full moon."

With her much fair speech she causeth him to yield,
With the flattering of her lips she forceth him away.
He goeth after her straightway,
As an ox goeth to the slaughter,
Or as fetters to the correction of the fool;
Till an arrow strike through his liver;
As a bird hasteth to the snare,
And knoweth not that it is for his life.

Now therefore, my sons, hearken unto me,
And attend to the words of my mouth.

[1] I.e., "I have a sacrificial feast at home." Sacrifice and feasting were inseparable.

Let not thine heart decline to her ways,
Go not astray in her paths.
For she hath cast down many wounded:
Yea, all her slain are a mighty host.
Her house is the way to Sheol,
Going down to the chambers of death.

The Proverbs of Solomon

A wise son maketh a glad father:
But a foolish son is the heaviness of his mother.

Hatred stirreth up strifes:
But love covereth all transgressions.

In the multitude of words there wanteth not transgression:
But he that refraineth his lips doeth wisely.

As vinegar to the teeth, and as smoke to the eyes,
So is the sluggard to them that send him.

Where no wise guidance is, the people falleth:
But in the multitude of counsellors there is safety.

As a jewel of gold in a swine's snout,
So is a fair woman which is without discretion.

Whoso loveth correction loveth knowledge:
But he that hateth reproof is brutish.

A virtuous woman is a crown to her husband:
But she that maketh ashamed is as rottenness in his bones.

A righteous man regardeth the life of his beast:
But the tender mercies of the wicked are cruel.

A fool's vexation is presently known:
But a prudent man concealeth shame.

A prudent man concealeth knowledge:
But the heart of fools proclaimeth foolishness.

The hand of the diligent shall bear rule:
But the slothful shall be put under taskwork.

There is that maketh himself rich, yet hath nothing:
There is that maketh himself poor, yet hath great wealth.

Hope deferred maketh the heart sick:
But when the desire cometh, it is a tree of life.

He that spareth his rod hateth his son:
But he that loveth him chasteneth him betimes.

The heart knoweth its own bitterness;
And a stranger doth not intermeddle with its joy.

There is a way which seemeth right unto a man,
But the end thereof are the ways of death.

Even in laughter the heart is sorrowful;
And the end of mirth is heaviness.

The simple believeth every word:
But the prudent man looketh well to his going.

The poor is hated even of his own neighbor;
But the rich hath many friends.

He that is slow to anger is of great understanding:
But he that is hasty of spirit exalteth folly.

A sound heart is the life of the flesh:
But envy is the rottenness of the bones.

A soft answer turneth away wrath:
But a grievous word stirreth up anger.

A merry heart maketh a cheerful countenance:
But by sorrow of heart the spirit is broken.

Better is a dinner of herbs where love is,
Than a stalled ox [2] and hatred therewith.

Pride goeth before destruction,
And a haughty spirit before a fall.

[2] **stalled ox** fatted ox, i.e., a rich dinner

Pleasant words are as a honeycomb,
Sweet to the soul, and health to the bones.

Better is a dry morsel and quietness therewith,
Than a house full of feasting with strife.

Whoso mocketh the poor reproacheth his Maker:
And he that is glad at calamity shall not be unpunished.

Let a bear robbed of her whelps meet a man,
Rather than a fool in his folly.

A friend loveth at all times,
And a brother is born for adversity.

Even a fool, when he holdeth his peace, is counted wise:
When he shutteth his lips, he is esteemed as prudent.

He also that is slack in his work
Is brother to him that is a destroyer.

A brother offended is harder to be won than a strong city:
And such contentions are like the bars of a castle.

The poor useth entreaties:
But the rich answereth roughly.

He that maketh many friends doeth it to his own destruction:
But there is a friend that sticketh closer than a brother.

Wealth addeth many friends:
But the poor is separated from his friend.

Many will intreat the favour of the liberal man:
And every man is a friend to him that giveth gifts.

House and riches are an inheritance from fathers:
But a prudent wife is from the Lord.

"It is naught, it is naught," saith the buyer:
But when he is gone his way, then he boasteth.

A good name is rather to be chosen than great riches,
And loving favour rather than silver and gold.

The rich and the poor meet together:
The Lord is the maker of them all.

Train up a child in the way he should go,
And even when he is old he will not depart from it.

Withhold not correction from the child:
For if thou beat him with the rod, he shall not die.
Thou shalt beat him with the rod,
And shalt deliver his soul from Sheol.

"WHO HATH WOE?"

Who hath woe? who hath sorrow? who hath contentions?
Who hath complaining? who hath wounds without cause?
Who hath redness of eyes?
They that tarry long at the wine;
They that go to seek out mixed wine.

Look not thou upon the wine when it is red,
When it giveth its colour in the cup,
When it goeth down smoothly:
At the last it biteth like a serpent,
And stingeth like an adder.
Thine eyes shall behold strange things,
And thine heart shall utter froward things.
Yea, thou shalt be as he that lieth down in the midst of the
        sea,
Or as he that lieth upon the top of a mast.
"They have stricken me," shalt thou say, "and I was not
        hurt;
They have beaten me, and I felt it not:
When shall I awake? I will seek it yet again."

The Hezekiah Collection

A word fitly spoken
Is like apples of gold in baskets of silver.

Let thy foot be seldom in thy neighbour's house;
Lest he be weary of thee, and hate thee.

Confidence in an unfaithful man in time of trouble
Is like a broken tooth, and a foot out of joint.

If thine enemy be hungry, give him bread to eat;
And if he be thirsty, give him water to drink:
For thou shalt heap coals of fire upon his head,
And the Lord shall reward thee.

It is better to dwell in the corner of the housetop,
Than with a contentious woman in a wide house.

He whose spirit is without restraint
Is like a city that is broken down and hath no wall.

The sluggard saith, "There is a lion in the way!
A lion is in the streets!"
As the door turneth upon its hinges,
So doth the sluggard upon his bed.
The sluggard burieth his hand in the dish;
It wearieth him to bring it again to his mouth.
The sluggard is wiser in his own conceit
Than seven men that can render a reason.

He that passeth by, and vexeth himself with strife belonging
    not to him,
Is like one that taketh a dog by the ears.

As a madman who casteth firebrands,
Arrows, and death;
So is the man that deceiveth his neighbour,
And saith, "Am not I in sport?"

For lack of wood the fire goeth out:
And where there is no whisper, contention ceaseth.

Boast not thyself of tomorrow;
For thou knowest not what a day may bring forth.

Let another man praise thee, and not thine own mouth;
A stranger and not thine own lips.

Wrath is cruel, and anger is outrageous;
But who is able to stand before jealousy.

He that blesseth his friend with a loud voice, rising early in
    the morning,
It shall be counted a curse to him.

A continual dropping in a very rainy day
And a contentious woman are alike:
He that would restrain her restraineth the wind,
And his right hand encountereth oil.

Iron sharpeneth iron;
So a man sharpeneth the countenance of his friend.

As in water face answereth to face,
So the heart of man to man.

The wicked flee when no man pursueth:
But the righteous are bold as a lion.

The Words of Agur

Two things have I asked of thee;
Deny me them not before I die:
Remove far from me vanity and lies:
Give me neither poverty nor riches;
Feed me with the food that is needful for me:
Lest I be full, and deny thee, and say, "Who is the Lord?"
Or lest I be poor, and steal,
And use profanely the name of my God.

There is a generation that curseth their father,
And doth not bless their mother.
There is a generation that are pure in their own eyes,
And yet are not washed from their filthiness.

There is a generation, oh how lofty are their eyes!
And their eyelids are lifted up.
There is a generation whose teeth are as swords, and their
        jaw teeth as knives,
To devour the poor from off the earth, and the needy from
        among men.

The horseleach hath two daughters, crying, "Give, give."
There are three things that are never satisfied,

Yea, four that say not, "Enough":
The grave; and the barren womb;
The earth that is not satisfied with water;
And the fire that saith not, "Enough."

There be three things which are too wonderful for me,
Yea, four which I know not:
The way of an eagle in the air;
The way of a serpent upon a rock;
The way of a ship in the midst of the sea;
And the way of a man with a maid.

For three things the earth doth tremble,
And for four, which it cannot bear:
For a servant when he is king;
And a fool when he is filled with meat;
For an odious woman when she is married;
And a handmaid that is heir to her mistress.

There be four things which are little upon the earth,
But they are exceeding wise:
The ants are a people not strong,
Yet they provide their meat in the summer;
The conies are but a feeble folk,
Yet make they their houses in the rocks;
The locusts have no king,
Yet go they forth all of them by bands;
The lizard taketh hold with her hands,
Yet is she in kings' palaces.

There be three things which are stately in their march,
Yea, four which are stately in going:
The lion, which is mightiest among beasts,
And turneth not away for any;
The greyhound; the he-goat also;
And the king, against whom there is no rising up.

The Book of
JOB

Prologue

THERE was a man in the land of Uz, whose name was Job; and that man was perfect and upright, and one that feared God, and eschewed evil. And there were born unto him seven sons and three daughters. His substance also was seven thousand sheep, and three thousand camels, and five hundred yoke of oxen, and five hundred she-asses, and a very great household; so that this man was the greatest of all the children of the east. And his sons went and held a feast in the house of each one upon his day; and they sent and called for their three sisters to eat and to drink with them. And it was so, when the days of their feasting were gone about, that Job sent and sanctified them, and rose up early in the morning, and offered burnt offerings according to the number of them all: for Job said,

> "It may be that my sons have sinned,
> And renounced God in their hearts."

Thus did Job continually.

Now there was a day when the sons of God came to present themselves before the Lord, and Satan came also among them. And the Lord said unto Satan,
"Whence comest thou?"
Then Satan answered the Lord, and said,

> "From going to and fro in the earth,
> And from walking up and down in it."

And the Lord said unto Satan,

"Hast thou considered by servant Job?
For there is none like him in the earth,
A perfect and an upright man,
One that feareth God, and escheweth evil."

Then Satan answered the Lord, and said,

"Doth Job fear God for nought?
Hast not thou made a hedge about him,
And about his house, and about all that he hath, on every
  side?
Thou hast blessed the work of his hands,
And his substance is increased in the land.
But put forth thine hand now,
And touch all that he hath,
And he will renounce thee to thy face."

And the Lord said unto Satan,

"Behold, all that he hath is in thy power;
Only upon himself put not forth thine hand."

So Satan went forth from the presence of the Lord.
And it fell on a day when his sons and his daughters were
eating and drinking wine in their eldest brother's house, that
there came a messenger unto Job, and said,

"The oxen were plowing,
And the asses feeding beside them:
And the Sabeans fell upon them, and took them away;
Yea, they have slain the servants with the edge of the
  sword;
And I only am escaped alone to tell thee."

While he was yet speaking, there came also another, and
said,

"The fire of God is fallen from heaven,
And hath burned up the sheep, and the servants, and
  consumed them;
And I only am escaped alone to tell thee."

While he was yet speaking, there came also another, and
said,

'The Chaldeans made three bands,
　And fell upon the camels, and have taken them away,
　Yea, and slain the servants with the edge of the sword;
　And I only am escaped alone to tell thee."

While he was yet speaking, there came also another, and
said,

"Thy sons and thy daughters were eating
　And drinking wine in their eldest brother's house:
　And, behold, there came a great wind from the wilderness,
　And smote the four corners of the house,
　And it fell upon the young men, and they are dead;
　And I only am escaped alone to tell thee."

Then Job arose, and rent his mantle, and shaved his head,
and fell down upon the ground, and worshipped; and he
said,

"Naked came I out of my mother's womb,
　And naked shall I return thither:
　The Lord gave, and the Lord hath taken away;
　Blessed be the name of the Lord."

In all this Job sinned not, nor charged God with foolishness.

Again there was a day when the sons of God came to
present themselves before the Lord, and Satan came also
among them to present himself before the Lord. And the
Lord said unto Satan,

"From whence comest thou?"

And Satan answered the Lord, and said,

"From going to and fro in the earth,
　And from walking up and down in it."

And the Lord said unto Satan,

"Hast thou considered my servant Job?
For there is none like him in the earth,
A perfect and an upright man,
One that feareth God, and escheweth evil:
And he still holdeth fast his integrity,
Although thou movedst me against him, to destroy him
   without cause."

And Satan answered the Lord, and said,

"Skin for skin!
 Yea, all that a man hath will he give for his life.
 But put forth thine hand now,
 And touch his bone and his flesh,
 And he will renounce thee to thy face."

And the Lord said unto Satan, "Behold, he is in thine
hand; only spare his life."

So Satan went forth from the presence of the Lord, and
smote Job with sore boils from the sole of his foot unto his
crown. And he took him a potsherd to scrape himself withal;
and he sat among the ashes. Then said his wife unto him,

"Dost thou still hold fast thine integrity?
 Renounce God, and die."

But he said unto her,

"Thou speakest as one of the foolish women speaketh.
 What? shall we receive good at the hand of God,
 And shall we not receive evil?"

In all this did not Job sin with his lips.

Now when Job's three friends heard of all this evil that
was come upon him, they came every one from his own
place; Eliphaz the Temanite, and Bildad the Shuhite, and
Zophar the Naamathite: and they made an appointment together to come to bemoan him and to comfort him. And
when they lifted up their eyes afar off, and knew him not,
they lifted up their voice, and wept; and they rent every
one his mantle, and sprinkled dust upon their heads toward

heaven. So they sat down with him upon the ground seven days and seven nights, and none spoke a word unto him: for they saw that his grief was very great.

I

JOB. Let the day perish wherein I was born,
And the night which said, "There is a man child conceived."
Let that day be darkness;
Let not God regard it from above,
Neither let the light shine upon it.
Let darkness and the shadow of death claim it for their own;
Let a cloud dwell upon it;
Let all that maketh black the day terrify it.
As for that night, let thick darkness seize upon it:
Let it not rejoice among the days of the year;
Let it not come into the number of the months.
Lo, let that night be barren;
Let no joyful voice come therein.
Let them curse it that curse the day,
Who are ready to rouse up Leviathan.[1]
Let the stars of the twilight thereof be dark:
Let it look for light, but have none;
Neither let it behold the eyelids of the morning:
Because it shut not up the doors of my mother's womb,
Nor hid trouble from mine eyes.
Why died I not from the womb?
Why did I not give up the ghost when I came out of the
    belly?
Why did the knees receive me?
Or why the breasts, that I should suck?
For now should I have lain down and been quiet;
I should have slept; then had I been at rest:
With kings and counsellors of the earth,
Which built up waste places for themselves;
Or with princes that had gold,

[1] Obscure, but seems to allude to sorcerers who can conjure up Leviathan, here meaning the chaos-dragon (elsewhere called Rahab) whom the Creator overcame

Who filled their houses with silver:
Or as a hidden untimely birth I had not been;
As infants which never saw light.
There the wicked cease from troubling;
And there the weary be at rest.
There the prisoners are at ease together;
They hear not the voice of the taskmaster.
The small and great are there;
And the servant is free from his master.
Wherefore is light given to him that is in misery,
And life unto the bitter in soul;
Which long for death, but it cometh not;
And dig for it more than for hid treasures;
Which rejoice exceedingly,
And are glad, when they can find the grave?
Why is light given to a man whose way is hid,
And whom God hath hedged in?
For my sighing cometh before I eat,
And my roarings are poured out like water.
For the thing which I fear cometh upon me,
And that which I am afraid of cometh unto me.
I am not at ease, neither am I quiet, neither have I rest;
But trouble cometh.

    ELIPHAZ. If one essay to commune with thee, wilt thou
        be grieved?
But who can withhold himself from speaking?
Behold, thou hast instructed many,
And thou hast strengthened the weak hands.
Thy words have upheld him that was falling,
And thou hast confirmed the feeble knees.
But now it is come unto thee, and thou faintest;
It toucheth thee, and thou art troubled.
Is not thy fear of God thy confidence,
And thy hope the integrity of thy ways?
Remember, I pray thee, who ever perished, being innocent?
Or where were the upright cut off?
According as I have seen, they that plow iniquity,
And sow trouble, reap the same.
By the breath of God they perish,
And by the blast of his anger are they consumed.
Now a thing was secretly brought to me,

And mine ear received a whisper thereof.
In thoughts from the visions of the night,
When deep sleep falleth on men,
Fear came upon me, and trembling,
Which made all my bones to shake.
Then a spirit passed before my face;
The hair of my flesh stood up.
It stood still, but I could not discern the appearance thereof;
A form was before mine eyes:
There was silence, and I heard a voice, saying,
"Shall mortal man be more just than God?
Shall a man be more pure than his Maker?
Behold, he putteth no trust in his servants;
And his angels he chargeth with folly:
How much more them that dwell in houses of clay,
Whose foundation is in the dust,
Which are crushed before the moth!
Betwixt morning and evening they are destroyed:
They perish for ever without any regarding it.
Is not their tent-cord plucked up within them?
They die, and that without wisdom."
Call now; is there any that will answer thee?
And to which of the holy ones wilt thou turn?
For affliction cometh not forth of the dust,
Neither doth trouble spring out of the ground;
But man is born unto trouble,
As the sparks fly upward.
But as for me, I would seek unto God,
And unto God would I commit my cause:
Which doeth great things and unsearchable;
Marvellous things without number:
Who giveth rain upon the earth,
And sendeth waters upon the fields:
So that he setteth up on high those that be low;
And those which mourn are exalted to safety.
He frustrateth the devices of the crafty,
So that their hands cannot perform their enterprise.
He taketh the wise in their own craftiness:
And the counsel of the froward is carried headlong.
They meet with darkness in the daytime,
And grope at noonday as in the night.

But he saveth from the sword of their mouth,
Even the needy from the hand of the mighty.
So the poor hath hope,
And iniquity stoppeth her mouth.
Behold, happy is the man whom God correcteth:
Therefore despise not thou the chastening of the Almighty.
For he maketh sore, and bindeth up;
He woundeth, and his hands make whole.
He shall deliver thee in six troubles;
Yea, in seven there shall no evil touch thee.
In famine he shall redeem thee from death;
And in war from the power of the sword.
Thou shalt be hid from the scourge of the tongue;
Neither shalt thou be afraid of destruction when it cometh.
At destruction and dearth thou shalt laugh;
Neither shalt thou be afraid of the beasts of the earth.
For thou shalt be in league with the stones of the field;
And the beasts of the field shall be at peace with thee.
And thou shalt know that thy tent is in peace;
And thou shalt visit thy fold, and shalt miss nothing.
Thou shalt know also that thy seed shall be great,
And thine offspring as the grass of the earth.
Thou shalt come to thy grave in a full age,
Like as a shock of corn cometh in in its season.
Lo this, we have searched it, so it is;
Hear it, and know thou it for thy good.

JOB. Oh that my vexation were but weighed,
And my calamity laid in the balances together!
For now it would be heavier than the sand of the seas:
Therefore have my words been rash.
For the arrows of the Almighty are within me,
The poison whereof my spirit drinketh up:
The terrors of God do set themselves in array against me.
Doth the wild ass bray when he hath grass?
Or loweth the ox over his fodder?
Oh that I might have my request;
And that God would grant me the thing that I long for!
Even that it would please God to crush me;
That he would let loose his hand, and cut me off!
Then should I yet have comfort;
Yea, I would exult in pain that spareth not:

For I have not denied the words of the Holy One.
What is my strength, that I should wait?
And what is mine end, that I should be patient?
Is my strength the strength of stones?
Or is my flesh of brass?
Is it not that I have no help in me,
And that effectual working is driven quite from me?
To him that is ready to faint kindness should be showed
    from his friend;
Even to him that forsaketh the fear of the Almighty.
My brethren have dealt deceitfully as a brook,
As the channel of brooks that pass away;
Which are black by reason of the ice,
And wherein the snow hideth itself:
What time they wax warm, they vanish:
When it is hot, they are consumed out of their place.
The caravans that travel by the way of them turn aside;
They go up into the waste, and perish.
The caravans of Tema looked,
The companies of Sheba waited for them.
They were ashamed because they had hoped;
They came thither, and were confounded.
For now ye are nothing;
Ye see a terror, and are afraid.
Did I say, "Give unto me?"
Or, "Offer a present for me of your substance?"
Or, "Deliver me from the adversary's hand?"
Or, "Redeem me from the hand of the oppressors?"
Teach me, and I will hold my peace:
And cause me to understand wherein I have erred.
How forcible are words of uprightness!
But what doth your arguing reprove?
Do ye imagine to reprove words?
Seeing that the speeches of one that is desperate are as wind.
Now therefore be pleased to look upon me;
For surely I shall not lie to your face.
Return, I pray you, let there be no injustice;
Yea, return again, my cause is righteous.
Is there injustice on my tongue?
Cannot my taste discern mischievous things?

Is there not a warfare to man upon earth?
And are not his days like the days of a hireling?
As a servant that earnestly desireth the shadow,
And as a hireling that looketh for his wages:
So am I made to possess months of vanity,[2]
And wearisome nights are appointed to me.
When I lie down, I say,
"When shall I arise?" but the night is long;
And I am full of tossings to and fro unto the dawning of the
        day.
My flesh is clothed with worms and clods of dust;
My skin closeth up and breaketh out afresh.
My days are swifter than a weaver's shuttle,
And are spent without hope.
Oh remember that my life is wind:
Mine eyes shall no more see good.
The eye of him that seeth me shall behold me no more·
Thine eyes shall be upon me, but I shall not be.
As the cloud is consumed and vanisheth away,
So he that goeth down to Sheol shall come up no more.
He shall return no more to his house,
Neither shall his place know him any more.
Therefore I will not refrain my mouth;
I will speak in the anguish of my spirit;
I will complain in the bitterness of my soul.
Am I a sea, or a sea-monster,
That thou[3] settest a watch over me?
When I say, "My bed shall comfort me.
My couch shall ease my complaint";
Then thou scarest me with dreams,
And terrifiest me through visions:
So that my soul chooseth strangling,
And death rather than these my bones.
I loathe my life; I would not live always:
Let me alone; for my days are vanity.
What is man, that thou shouldest magnify him,
And that thou shouldest set thine heart upon him,
And that thou shouldest visit him every morning,
And try him every moment?

[2] **vanity** emptiness   [3] **thou** God

How long wilt thou not look away from me,
Nor let me alone till I swallow down my spittle?
If I have sinned, what do I unto thee, O thou watcher of
　　men?
Why hast thou set me as a mark for thee,
So that I am a burden to myself?
And why dost thou not pardon my transgression, and take
　　away mine iniquity?
For now shall I lie down in the dust;
And thou shalt seek me diligently, but I shall not be.
　　BILDAD. How long wilt thou speak these things?
And how long shall the words of thy mouth be like a mighty
　　wind?
Doth God pervert judgment?
Or doth the Almighty pervert justice?
If thy children have sinned against him,
And he have delivered them into the hand of their trans-
　　gression:
If thou wouldest seek diligently unto God,
And make thy supplication to the Almighty;
If thou wert pure and upright;
Surely now he would awake for thee,
And make the habitation of thy righteousness prosperous.
And though thy beginning was small,
Yet thy latter end should greatly increase.
For inquire, I pray thee, of the former age,
And apply thyself to that which their fathers have searched
　　out
(For we are but of yesterday, and know nothing,
Because our days upon earth are a shadow):
Shall not they teach thee, and tell thee,
And utter words out of their heart?
Can the rush grow up without mire?
Can the flag grow without water?
Whilst it is yet in its greenness, and not cut down,
It withereth before any other herb.
So are the paths of all that forget God;
And the hope of the godless man shall perish:
Whose confidence shall break in sunder,
And whose trust is a spider's web.

He shall lean upon his house,[4] but it shall not stand:
He shall hold fast thereby, but it shall not endure.
He is green before the sun,
And his shoots go forth over his garden.
If he be destroyed from his place,
Then it shall deny him, saying, "I have not seen thee."
Behold, this is the joy of his way,
And out of the earth shall others spring.
Behold, God will not cast away a perfect man,
Neither will he uphold the evildoers.
He will yet fill thy mouth with laughter,
And thy lips with shouting.
They that hate thee shall be clothed with shame;
And the tent of the wicked shall be no more.

JOB. Of a truth I know that it is so:
But how can man be just with God?
If he be pleased to contend with him,[5]
He cannot answer him one of a thousand.
He is wise in heart, and mighty in strength:
Who hath hardened himself against him, and prospered?
Which removeth the mountains, and they know it not,
When he overturneth them in his anger.
Which shaketh the earth out of her place,
And the pillars thereof tremble.
Which commandeth the sun, and it riseth not;
And sealeth up the stars.
Which alone stretcheth out the heavens,
And treadeth upon the waves of the sea.
Which maketh the Bear, Orion, and the Pleiades,
And the chambers of the south.[6]
Which doeth great things past finding out;
Yea, marvellous things without number.
Lo, he goeth by me, and I see him not:
He passeth on also, but I perceive him not.
Behold, he seizeth the prey, who can hinder him?
Who will say unto him, "What doest thou?"
God will not withdraw his anger;

[4] **his house** the spider's web [5] Read: "If one desires to argue with God" . . . [6] Meaning unknown

The helpers of Rahab [7] do stoop under him.
How much less shall I answer him,
And choose out my words to reason with him?
Whom, though I were righteous, yet would I not answer;
I would make supplication to mine adversary.
If I had called, and he had answered me;
Yet would I not believe that he hearkened unto my voice.
For he breaketh me with a tempest,
And multiplieth my wounds without cause.
He will not suffer me to take my breath,
But filleth me with bitterness.
Though I be righteous, mine own mouth shall condemn me:
Though I be perfect, it shall prove me perverse.
I am perfect; I regard not myself;
I despise my life.
It is all one; therefore I say,
He destroyeth the perfect and the wicked.
If the scourge slay suddenly,
He will mock at the trial of the innocent.
The earth is given into the hand of the wicked:
He covereth the faces of the judges thereof;
If it be not he, who then is it?
Now my days are swifter than a post:
They flee away, they see no good.
They are passed away as the swift ships:
As the eagle that swoopeth on the prey.
If I say, "I will forget my complaint,
I will put off my sad countenance, and be of good cheer":
I am afraid of all my sorrows,
I know that thou wilt not hold me innocent.
I shall be condemned;
Why then do I labour in vain?
If I wash myself with snow water,
And make my hands never so clean;
Yet wilt thou plunge me in the ditch,
And mine own clothes shall abhor me.
For he is not a man, as I am, that I should answer him,
That we should come together in judgment.
There is no daysman [8] betwixt us,

[7] **Rahab** in Babylonian lore the guardian monster of chaos.
See note 1.   [8] **daysman**, arbiter

That might lay his hand upon us both.
Let him take his rod away from me,
And let not his terror make me afraid:
Then would I speak, and not fear him;
For I am not so in myself.

My soul is weary of my life;
I will give free course to my complaint;
I will speak in the bitterness of my soul.
I will say unto God, "Do not condemn me;
Show me wherefore thou contendest with me.
Is it good unto thee that thou shouldest oppress,
That thou shouldest despise the work of thine hands,
And shine upon the counsel of the wicked?
Hast thou eyes of flesh,
Or seest thou as man seeth?
Are thy days as the days of man,
Or thy years as man's days,
That thou inquirest after mine iniquity,
And searchest after my sin,
Although thou knowest that I am not wicked;
And there is none that can deliver out of thine hand?
Thine hands have framed me and fashioned me
Together round about; yet thou dost destroy me.
Remember, I beseech thee, that thou hast fashioned me as
    clay;
And wilt thou bring me into dust again?
Hast thou not poured me out as milk,
And curdled me like cheese?
Thou hast clothed me with skin and flesh,
And knit me together with bones and sinews.
Thou has granted me life and favour,
And thy visitation hath preserved my spirit.
Yet these things thou didst hide in thine heart;
I know that this is with thee:
If I sin, then thou markest me,
And thou wilt not acquit me from mine iniquity.
If I be wicked, woe unto me;
And if I be righteous, yet shall I not lift up my head;
Being filled with ignominy
And looking upon mine affliction.

And if my head exalt itself, thou huntest me as a lion:
And again thou showest thyself marvellous upon me.
Thou renewest thy witnesses against me,
And increasest thine indignation upon me;
Changes and warfare are with me.
Wherefore then hast thou brought me forth out of the
   womb?
I had given up the ghost, and no eye had seen me.
I should have been as though I had not been;
I should have been carried from the womb to the grave.
Are not my days few? cease then,
And let me alone, that I may take comfort a little,
Before I go whence I shall not return,
Even to the land of darkness and of the shadow of death;
A land of thick darkness, as darkness itself;
A land of the shadow of death, without any order,
And where the light is as darkness."

ZOPHAR. Should not the multitude of words be answered?
And should a man full of talk be justified?
Should thy boastings make men hold their peace?
And when thou mockest, shall no man make thee ashamed?
For thou sayest, "My doctrine is pure,
And I am clean in thine eyes."
But oh that God would speak,
And open his lips against thee;
And that he would show thee the secrets of wisdom,
That it is manifold in effectual working!
Know therefore that God exacteth of thee less than thine
   iniquity deserveth.
Canst thou by searching find out God?
Canst thou find out the Almighty unto perfection?
It is high as heaven; what canst thou do?
Deeper than Sheol; what canst thou know?
The measure thereof is longer than the earth,
And broader than the sea,
If he pass through, and shut up,
And call unto judgment, then who can hinder him?
For he knoweth vain men:
He seeth iniquity also, even though he consider it not.
But vain man is void of understanding,
Yea, man is born as a wild ass's colt.

If thou set thine heart aright,
And stretch out thine hands toward him;
If iniquity be in thine hand, put it far away,
And let not unrighteousness dwell in thy tents;
Surely then shalt thou lift up thy face without spot;
Yea, thou shalt be steadfast, and shalt not fear:
For thou shalt forget thy misery;
Thou shalt remember it as waters that are passed away:
And thy life shall be clearer than the noonday;
Though there be darkness, it shall be as the morning.
And thou shalt be secure, because there is hope;
Yea, thou shalt search about thee, and shalt take thy rest in
    safety.
Also thou shalt lie down, and none shall make thee afraid;
Yea, many shall make suit unto thee.
But the eyes of the wicked shall fail,
And they shall have no way to flee,
And their hope shall be the giving up of the ghost.

    JOB. No doubt but ye are the people,
And wisdom shall die with you.
But I have understanding as well as you;
I am not inferior to you:
Yea, who knoweth not such things as these?
I am as one that is a laughing-stock to his neighbour,
A man that called upon God, and he answered him:
The just, the perfect man is a laughing-stock.
In the thought of him that is at ease there is contempt for
    misfortune;
It is ready for them whose foot slippeth.
The tents of robbers prosper,
And they that provoke God are secure;
Into whose hand God bringeth abundantly.
But ask now the beasts, and they shall teach thee;
And the fowls of the air and they shall tell thee:
Or speak to the earth, and it shall teach thee;
And the fishes of the sea shall declare unto thee.
Who knoweth not in all these,
That the hand of the Lord hath wrought this?
In whose hand is the soul of every living thing,
And the breath of all mankind.

Lo, mine eye hath seen all this,
Mine ear hath heard and understood it.
What ye know, the same do I know also:
I am not inferior unto you.
Surely I would speak to the Almighty,
And I desire to reason with God.
But ye are forgers of lies,
Ye are all physicians of no value.
Oh that ye would altogether hold your peace!
And it should be your wisdom.
Hear now my reasoning,
And hearken to the pleadings of my lips.
Will ye speak unrighteously for God,
And talk deceitfully for him?
Will ye respect his person? [9]
Will ye contend for God?
Is it good that he should search you out?
Or as one deceiveth a man, will ye deceive him?
He will surely reprove you,
If ye do secretly respect persons.
Shall not his excellency make you afraid,
And his dread fall upon you?
Your memorable sayings are proverbs of ashes,
Your defences are defences of clay.
Hold your peace, let me alone, that I may speak,
And let come on me what will.
Wherefore should I take my flesh in my teeth,
And put my life in mine hand?
Though he slay me, yet will I wait for him:
Nevertheless I will maintain my ways before him.
This also shall be my salvation;
For a godless man shall not come before him.
Hear diligently my speech,
And let my declaration be in your ears.
Behold now, I have ordered my cause;
I know that I am righteous.
Who is he that will contend with me?
For now shall I hold my peace and give up the ghost.
Only do not two things unto me, [10]

[9] respect his person i.e., show partiality towards God   [10] Now
Job addresses God

Then will I not hide myself from thy face:
Withdraw thine hand far from me;
And let not thy terror make me afraid.
Then call thou, and I will answer;
Or let me speak, and answer thou me.
How many are mine iniquities and sins?
Make me to know my transgression and my sin.
Wherefore hidest thou thy face,
And holdest me for thine enemy?
Wilt thou harass a driven leaf?
And wilt thou pursue the dry stubble?
For thou writest bitter things against me,
And makest me to inherit the iniquities of my youth:
Thou puttest my feet also in the stocks, and markest all
    my paths;
Thou drawest thee a line about the soles of my feet:
Though I am like a rotten thing that consumeth,
Like a garment that is moth-eaten.

Man that is born of a woman
Is of few days, and full of trouble.
He cometh forth like a flower, and is cut down:
He fleeth also as a shadow, and continueth not.
And dost thou open thine eyes upon such a one,
And bringest me into judgment with thee?
Who can bring a clean thing out of an unclean? not one.
Seeing his days are determined, the number of his months
    is with thee,
And thou hast appointed his bounds that he cannot pass;
Look away from him, that he may rest,
Till he shall accomplish, as a hireling, his day.
For there is hope of a tree, if it be cut down, that it will
    sprout again,
And that the tender branch thereof will not cease.
Though the root thereof wax old in the earth,
And the stock thereof die in the ground;
Yet through the scent of water it will bud,
And put forth boughs like a plant.
But man dieth, and wasteth away:
Yea, man giveth up the ghost, and where is he?
As the waters fail from the sea,

And the river decayeth and drieth up;
So man lieth down and riseth not:
Till the heavens be no more, they shall not awake,
Nor be roused out of their sleep.
Oh that thou wouldest hide me in Sheol,
That thou wouldest keep me secret, until thy wrath be past,
That thou wouldest appoint me a set time, and remember
 me!
If a man die, shall he live again?
All the days of my warfare would I wait,
Till my release should come.
Thou shouldest call, and I would answer thee:
Thou wouldest have a desire to the work of thine hands.
But now thou numberest my steps:
Dost thou not watch over my sin?
My transgression is sealed up in a bag,
And thou fastenest up mine iniquity.
And surely the mountain falling cometh to nought,
And the rock is removed out of its place;
The waters wear the stones;
The overflowings thereof wash away the dust of the earth:
And thou destroyest the hope of man.
Thou prevailest for ever against him, and he passeth;
Thou changest his countenance, and sendest him away.
His sons come to honour, and he knoweth it not;
And they are brought low, but he perceiveth it not of them.
But his flesh upon him hath pain,
And his soul within him mourneth.

II

ELIPHAZ. Should a wise man make answer with vain
 knowledge,
And fill his belly with the east wind?
Should he reason with unprofitable talk,
Or with speeches wherewith he can do no good?
Yea, thou doest away with fear,
And restrainest devotion before God.
For thine iniquity teacheth thy mouth,

And thou choosest the tongue of the crafty.
Thine own mouth condemneth thee, and not I;
Yea, thine own lips testify against thee.
Art thou the first man that was born?
Or wast thou brought forth before the hills?
Hast thou heard the secret counsel of God?
And dost thou restrain wisdom to thyself?
What knowest thou, that we know not?
What understandest thou, which is not in us?
With us are both the grayheaded and the very aged men,
Much elder than thy father.
Are the consolations of God too small for thee,
And the word that dealeth gently with thee?
Why doth thine heart carry thee away?
And why do thine eyes wink?
That thou turnest thy spirit against God,
And lettest such words go out of thy mouth.
What is man, that he should be clean?
And he which is born of a woman, that he should be
  righteous?
Behold, he putteth no trust in his holy ones;
Yea, the heavens are not clean in his sight.
How much less one that is abominable and corrupt,
A man that drinketh iniquity like water!
I will show thee, hear thou me;
And that which I have seen I will declare
(Which wise men have told
From their fathers, and have not hid it;
Unto whom alone the land was given,
And no stranger passed among them):
The wicked man travaileth with pain all his days,
Even the number of years that are laid up for the oppressor.
A sound of terrors is in his ears;
In prosperity the spoiler shall come upon him:
He believeth not that he shall return out of darkness,
And he is waited for of the sword:
He wandereth abroad for bread, saying, "Where is it?"
He knoweth that the day of darkness is ready at his hand:
Distress and anguish make him afraid;

  JOB. I have heard many such things:
Miserable comforters are ye all.

Shall vain words have an end?
Or what provoketh thee that thou answerest?
I also could speak as ye do;
If your soul were in my soul's stead,
I could join words together against you,
And shake mine head at you.
But I would strengthen you with my mouth,
And the solace of my lips should assuage your grief.
Though I speak, my grief is not assuaged:
And though I forbear, what am I eased?
But now he hath made me weary:
Thou hast made desolate all my company.
And thou hast laid fast hold on me, which is a witness
    against me:
And my leanness riseth up against me, it testifieth to my
    face.
He hath torn me in his wrath, and persecuted me;
He hath gnashed upon me with his teeth:
Mine adversary sharpeneth his eyes upon me.
They have gaped upon me with their mouth;
They have smitten me upon the cheek reproachfully:
They gather themselves together against me.
God delivereth me to the ungodly,
And casteth me into the hands of the wicked.
I was at ease, and he broke me asunder;
Yea, he hath taken me by the neck, and dashed me to pieces:
He hath also set me up for his mark.
His archers compass me round about,
He cleaveth my reins asunder, and doth not spare;
He poureth out my gall upon the ground.
He breaketh me with breach upon breach;
He runneth upon me like a giant.
I have sewed sackcloth upon my skin,
And have laid my horn in the dust.
My face is foul with weeping,
And on my eyelids is the shadow of death;
Although there is no violence in mine hands,
And my prayer is pure.
O earth, cover not thou my blood,
And let my cry have no resting place.
Even now, behold, my witness is in heaven,

And he that voucheth for me is on high.
My friends scorn me:
But mine eye poureth out tears unto God;
That he would maintain the right of a man with God,
And of a son of man with his neighbour!
For when a few years are come,
I shall go the way whence I shall not return.

BILDAD. How long will ye lay snares for words?
Consider, and afterwards we will speak.
Wherefore are we counted as beasts,
And are become unclean in your sight?
Yea, the light of the wicked shall be put out,
And the spark of his fire shall not shine.
His remembrance shall perish from the earth,
And he shall have no name in the street.
He shall be driven from light into darkness,
And chased out of the world.
JOB. How long will ye vex my soul,
And break me in pieces with words?
These ten times have ye reproached me:
Ye are not ashamed that ye deal hardly with me.
And be it indeed that I have erred,
Mine error remaineth with myself.
If indeed ye will magnify yourselves against me,
And plead against me my reproach:
Know now that God hath subverted me in my cause,
And hath compassed me with his net.
Behold, I cry out of wrong, but I am not heard:
I cry for help, but there is no judgment.
He hath fenced up my way that I cannot pass.
And hath set darkness in my paths.
He hath stripped me of my glory,
And taken the crown from my head.
He hath put my brethren far from me,
And mine acquaintance are wholly estranged from me.
My kinsfolk have failed,
And my familiar friends have forgotten me.
They that dwell in mine house, and my maids, count me
    for a stranger:
I am an alien in their sight.

I call unto my servant, and he giveth me no answer,
Though I intreat him with my mouth.
My breath is strange to my wife,
And my supplication to the children of my mother's womb.
Even young children despise me;
If I arise, they speak against me.
All my inward friends abhor me:
And they whom I loved are turned against me.
My bone cleaveth to my skin and to my flesh,
And I am escaped with the skin of my teeth.
Have pity upon me, have pity upon me, O ye my friends;
For the hand of God hath touched me.
Why do ye persecute me as God,
And are not satisfied with my flesh?
Oh that my words were now written!
Oh that they were inscribed in a book!
That with an iron pen and lead
They were graven in the rock for ever!
But I know that my redeemer liveth,
And that he shall stand up at the last upon the earth:
And after my skin hath been thus destroyed,
Yet from my flesh shall I see God:
Whom I shall see for myself,
And mine eyes shall behold, and not another.

   Zophar. I have heard the reproof which putteth me to
     shame,
And the spirit of my understanding answereth me.
Knowest thou not this of old time,
Since man was placed upon earth,
That the triumphing of the wicked is short,
And the joy of the godless but for a moment?
Though his excellency mount up to the heavens,
And his head reach unto the clouds;
Yet he shall perish for ever like his own dung:
They which have seen him shall say, "Where is he?"
He shall fly away as a dream, and shall not be found:
Yea, he shall be chased away as a vision of the night.
The eye which saw him shall see him no more;
Neither shall his place any more behold him.
For he hath oppressed and forsaken the poor;

He hath violently taken away a house, and he shall not
    build it up.
Because he knew no quietness within him,
He shall not save aught of that wherein he delighteth.
There was nothing left that he devoured not;
Therefore his prosperity shall not endure.
In the fulness of his sufficiency he shall be in straits:
The hand of every one that is in misery shall come upon
    him.
This is the portion of a wicked man from God,
And the heritage appointed unto him by God.

    JOB. Hear diligently my speech;
And let this be your consolations.
Suffer me, and I also will speak;
And after that I have spoken, mock on.
As for me, is my complaint to man?
And why should I not be impatient?
Mark me, and be astonished,
And lay your hand upon your mouth.
Even when I remember I am troubled,
And horror taketh hold on my flesh.
Wherefore do the wicked live,
Become old, yea, wax mighty in power?
Their seed is established with them in their sight,
And their offspring before their eyes.
Their houses are safe from fear,
Neither is the rod of God upon them.
Their bull gendereth, and faileth not;
Their cow calveth, and casteth not her calf.
They send forth their little ones like a flock,
And their children dance.
They sing to the timbrel and harp,
And rejoice at the sound of the pipe.
They spend their days in prosperity,
And in a moment they go down to Sheol.
Yet they said unto God, "Depart from us!
For we desire not the knowledge of thy ways.
What is the Almighty, that we should serve him?
And what profit should we have, if we pray unto him?"
How oft is it that the lamp of the wicked is put out?
That their calamity cometh upon them?

That God distributeth sorrow in his anger?
That they are as stubble before the wind,
And as chaff that the storm carrieth away?
One dieth in his full strength,
Being wholly at ease and quiet:
His breasts are full of milk,
And the marrow of his bones is moistened.
And another dieth in bitterness of soul,
And never tasteth of good.
They lie down alike in the dust,
And the worm covereth them.
How then comfort ye me in vain,
Seeing in your answers there remaineth only falsehood?

III

ELIPHAZ. Can a man be profitable unto God?
Surely he that is wise is profitable unto himself.
Is it any pleasure to the Almighty, that thou art righteous?
Or is it gain to him, that thou makest thy ways perfect?
Is it for thy fear of him that he reproveth thee,
That he enter with thee into judgment?
Is not thy wickedness great? [11]
Neither is there any end to thine iniquities.
For thou hast taken pledges of thy brother for nought,
And stripped the naked of their clothing.
Thou hast not given water to the weary to drink,
And thou hast withheld bread from the hungry.
Thou hast sent widows away empty,
And the arms of the fatherless have been broken.
Therefore snares are round about thee,
And sudden fear troubleth thee,
Or darkness, that thou canst not see,
And abundance of waters cover thee.
Is not God in the height of heaven?

[11] Eliphaz is now willing to conclude Job a sinner, according to the belief of the time that suffering results from sin as prosperity results from virtue. He therefore accuses Job of specific (though unproved) sins.

And behold the height of the stars, how high they are!
And thou sayest, "What doth God know?
Can he judge through the thick darkness?"
Thick clouds are a covering to him, that he seeth not;
And he walketh in the circuit of heaven.
Wilt thou keep the old way
Which wicked men have trodden?
Who were snatched away before their time,
Whose foundation was poured out as a stream.
Acquaint now thyself with him, and be at peace:
Thereby good shall come unto thee.
Receive, I pray thee, the law from his mouth,
And lay up his words in thine heart.
If thou return to the Almighty, thou shalt be built up;
If thou put away unrighteousness far from thy tents.
And lay thou thy treasure in the dust,
And the gold of Ophir among the stones of the brooks;
And the Almighty shall be thy treasure,
And precious silver unto thee.
For then shalt thou delight thyself in the Almighty,
And shalt lift up thy face unto God.
Thou shalt make thy prayer unto him, and he shall hear
    thee;
And thou shalt pay thy vows.
Thou shalt also decree a thing, and it shall be established
    unto thee;
And light shall shine upon thy ways.
When they cast thee down, thou shalt say, "There is lifting
    up";
And the humble person he shall save.

   Job. Even to-day is my complaint rebellious:
My stroke is heavier than my groaning.
Oh that I knew where I might find him,
That I might come even to his seat!
I would order my cause before him,
And fill my mouth with arguments.
I would know the words which he would answer me,
And understand what he would say unto me.
Would he contend with me in the greatness of his power?
Nay; but he would give heed unto me.
There the upright might reason with him;

So should I be delivered for ever from my judge.
Behold, I go forward, but he is not there;
And backward, but I cannot perceive him:
On the left hand, when he doth work, but I cannot behold
    him:
He hideth himself on the right hand, that I cannot see him.
But he knoweth the way that I take;
When he hath tried me, I shall come forth as gold.
My foot hath held fast to his steps;
His way have I kept, and turned not aside.
I have not gone back from the commandment of his lips;
I have treasured up the words of his mouth more than my
    necessary food.
But he is in one mind, and who can turn him?
And what his soul desireth, even that he doeth.
For he performeth that which is appointed for me:
And many such things are with him.
Therefore am I troubled at his presence;
When I consider, I am afraid of him.
For God hath made my heart faint,
And the Almighty hath troubled me.

    BILBAD. Dominion and fear are with him;
He maketh peace in his high places.
Is there any number of his armies?
And upon whom doth not his light arise?
How then can man be just with God?
Or how can he be clean that is born of a woman?
Behold, even the moon hath no brightness,
And the stars are not pure in his sight:
How much less man, that is a worm!
And the son of man, which is a worm!

    JOB. How hast thou helped him that is without power!
How hast thou saved the arm that hath no strength!
How hast thou counselled him that hath no wisdom,
And plentifully declared sound knowledge!
To whom hast thou uttered words?
And whose spirit came forth from thee?
As God liveth, who hath taken away my right;
And the Almighty, who hath vexed my soul
Surely my lips shall not speak unrighteousness,
Neither shall my tongue utter deceit.

God forbid that I should justify you:
Till I die I will not put away mine integrity from me.
My righteousness I hold fast, and will not let it go:
My heart shall not reproach me so long as I live.

ZOPHAR.[12] Let mine enemy be as the wicked,
And let him that riseth up against me be as the unrighteous
For what is the hope of the godless, though he get him gain,
When God taketh away his soul?
Will God hear his cry,
When trouble cometh upon him?
Will he delight himself in the Almighty,
And call upon God at all times?

JOB. Oh that I were as in the months of old,
As in the days when God watched over me;
When his lamp shined upon my head,
And by his light I walked through darkness;
As I was in the ripeness of my days,
When the secret of God was upon my tent;
When the Almighty was yet with me,
And my children were about me;
When my steps were washed with butter,
And the rock poured me out rivers of oil!
When I went forth to the gate unto the city,
When I prepared my seat in the street,
The young men saw me and hid themselves,
And the aged rose up and stood;
The princes refrained talking,
And laid their hand on their mouth;
The voice of the nobles was hushed,
And their tongue cleaved to the roof of their mouth.
For when the ear heard me, then it blessed me;
And when the eye saw me, it gave witness unto me:
Because I delivered the poor that cried,
The fatherless also, that had none to help him.
The blessing of him that was ready to perish came upon me:
And I caused the widow's heart to sing for joy.
I put on righteousness, and it clothed me:
My justice was as a robe and a diadem.

[12] Although originally assigned to Job, this speech is not consistent with his views. Many scholars therefore assign it to Zophar, as here

I was eyes to the blind,
And feet was I to the lame.
I was a father to the needy:
And the cause of him that I knew not I searched out.
And I broke the jaws of the unrighteous,
And plucked the prey out of his teeth.
Then I said, "I shall die in my nest,
And I shall multiply my days as the sand:
My root is spread out to the waters,
And the dew lieth all night upon my branch:
My glory is fresh in me,
And my bow is renewed in my hand."
Unto me men gave ear, and waited,
And kept silence for my counsel.
After my words they spoke not again;
And my speech dropped upon them.
And they waited for me as for the rain;
And they opened their mouth wide as for the latter rain.

But now they that are younger than I have me in derision,
Whose fathers I disdained to set with the dogs of my flock.
And now I am become their song,
Yea, I am a byword unto them.
They abhor me, they stand aloof from me,
And spare not to spit in my face.
Terrors are turned upon me,
They chase mine honour as the wind;
And my welfare is passed away as a cloud.
I cry unto thee, and thou dost not answer me:
I stand up, and thou lookest at me.
Thou art turned to be cruel to me:
With the might of thy hand thou persecutest me.
Thou liftest me up to the wind, thou causest me to ride
    upon it;
And thou dissolvest me in the storm.
For I know that thou wilt bring me to death,
And to the house appointed for all living.
Surely against a ruinous heap he will not put forth his hand;
Though it be in his destruction, one may utter a cry because
    of these things.
Did not I weep for him that was in trouble?

Was not my soul grieved for the needy?
When I looked for good, then evil came;
And when I waited for light, there came darkness.
Therefore is my harp turned to mourning,
And my pipe into the voice of them than weep.

Doth not he see my ways,
And number all my steps?
If I have walked with vanity,
And my foot hath hastened to deceit
(Let me be weighed in an even balance,
That God may know mine integrity);
If my step hath turned out of the way,
And mine heart walked after mine eyes,
And if any spot hath cleaved to mine hands:
Then let me sow, and let another eat;
Yea, let the produce of my field be rooted out.
If mine heart have been enticed unto a woman,
And I have laid wait at my neighbour's door:
Then let my wife grind unto another,[13]
And let others bow down upon her.
If I did despise the cause of my manservant or of my maid-
    servant
When they contended with me:
What then shall I do when God riseth up?
And when he visiteth, what shall I answer him?
Did not he that made me in the womb make him?
And did not one fashion us in the womb?
If I have withheld the poor from their desire,
Or have caused the eyes of the widow to fail;
Or have eaten my morsel alone,
And the fatherless hath not eaten thereof;
If I have seen any perish for want of clothing,
Or that the needy had no covering;
If his loins[14] have not blessed me,
And if he were not warmed with the fleece of my sheep;
If I have lifted up my hand against the fatherless,

[13] Let my wife grind another person's grain, i.e., be a servant
or slave [14] **loins** we would say *heart*. The ancients considered
the kidneys the seat of the affections.

Because I saw my help in the gate: [15]
Then let my shoulder fall from the shoulder blade,
And mine arm be broken from the bone.
If I have made gold my hope,
And have said to the fine gold, "Thou art my confidence";
If I rejoiced because my wealth was great,
And because mine hand had gotten much;
If I beheld the sun when it shined,[16]
Or the moon walking in brightness;
And my heart hath been secretly enticed,
And my mouth hath kissed my hand:
This also were an iniquity to be punished by the judges:
For I should have lied to God that is above.
If I rejoiced at the destruction of him that hated me,
Or lifted up myself when evil found him
(Yea, I suffered not my mouth to sin
By asking his life with a curse);
If the men of my tent said not,
"Who can find one that hath not been satisfied with his
    flesh?"
The stranger did not lodge in the street;
But I opened my doors to the traveller;
If like Adam I covered my transgressions,
By hiding mine iniquity in my bosom;
Because I feared the great multitude,
And the contempt of families terrified me,
So that I kept silence, and went not out of the door—
Oh, that I had one to hear me!
(Lo, here is my signature, let the Almighty answer me);
And that I had the indictment which mine adversary hath
    written!
Surely I would carry it upon my shoulder;
I would bind it unto me as a crown.

[15] "my help in the gate." The gate of the city was the meeting place of the elders sitting in judgment. Job means that he has not taken advantage of the weak even if legally entitled to do so.   [16] "If I beheld the sun," etc. He has not been tempted to worship the heavenly bodies, whose cults competed seriously with that of Jehovah.

I would declare unto him the number of my steps;
As a prince would I go near unto him.

The words of Job are ended.

IV

VOICE OUT OF THE WHIRLWIND. Who is this that dark-
    eneth counsel
By words without knowledge?
Gird up now thy loins like a man;
For I will demand of thee, and declare thou unto me.
Where wast thou when I laid the foundations of the earth?
Declare, if thou hast understanding.
Who determined the measures thereof, if thou knowest?
Or who stretched the line upon it?
Whereupon were the foundations thereof fastened?
Or who laid the corner stone thereof;
When the morning stars sang together,
And all the sons of God shouted for joy?
Or who shut up the sea with doors,
When it broke forth, as if it had issued out of the womb;
When I made the cloud the garment thereof,
And thick darkness a swaddlingband for it,
And prescribed for it my decree,
And set bars and doors,
And said, "Hitherto shalt thou come, but no further;
And here shall thy proud waves be stayed"?
Hast thou commanded the morning since thy days began,
And caused the dayspring to know its place;
That it might take hold of the ends of the earth,
And the wicked be shaken out of it?
It is changed as clay under the seal;
And all things stand forth as a garment:
And from the wicked their light is withheld,
And the high arm is broken.
Hast thou entered into the springs of the sea?
Or hast thou walked in the recesses of the deep?
Have the gates of death been revealed unto thee?

Or hast thou seen the gates of the shadow of death?
Hast thou comprehended the breadth of the earth?
Declare, if thou knowest it all.
Where is the way to the dwelling of light,
And as for darkness, where is the place thereof;
That thou shouldest take it to the bound thereof,
And that thou shouldest discern the paths to the house
　　thereof?
Doubtless, thou knowest, for thou wast then born,
And the number of thy days is great!
Hast thou entered the treasuries of the snow,
Or hast thou seen the treasuries of the hail,
Which I have reserved against the time of trouble,
Against the day of battle and war?
By what way is the light parted,
Or the east wind scattered upon the earth?
Who hath cleft a channel for the waterflood,
Or a way for the lightning of the thunder;
To cause it to rain on a land where no man is;
On the wilderness, wherein there is no man;
To satisfy the waste and desolate ground;
And to cause the tender grass to spring forth?
Hath the rain a father?
Or who hath begotten the drops of dew?
Out of whose womb came the ice?
And the hoary frost of heaven, who hath gendered it?
The waters are hidden as with stone,
And the face of the deep is frozen.
Canst thou bind the cluster of the Pleiades,
Or loose the bands of Orion?
Canst thou lead forth the Mazzaroth [17] in their season?
Or canst thou guide the Bear with her train?
Knowest thou the ordinances of the heavens?
Canst thou establish the dominion thereof in the earth?
Canst thou lift up thy voice to the clouds,
That abundance of waters may cover thee?
Canst thou send forth lightnings, that they may go,
And say unto thee, "Here we are"?

[17] **Mazzaroth** meaning unknown, but probably refers to some
heavenly constellation

Who hath put wisdom in the inward parts?
Or who hath given understanding to the mind?
Who can number the clouds by wisdom?
Or who can pour out the bottles of heaven,
When the dust runneth into a mass,
And the clods cleave fast together?
Wilt thou hunt the prey for the lioness?
Or satisfy the appetite of the young lions,
When they couch in their dens,
And abide in the covert to lie in wait?
Who provideth for the raven his food,
When his young ones cry unto God,
And wander for lack of meat?

Knowest thou the time when the wild goats of the rock
    bring forth?
Or canst thou mark when the hinds do calve?
Canst thou number the months that they fulfil?
Or knowest thou the time when they bring forth?
They bow themselves, they bring forth their young,
They cast out their sorrows.
Their young ones are in good liking, they grow up in the
    open field;
They go forth, and return not again.
    Who hath sent out the wild ass free?
Or who hath loosed the bands of the wild ass?
Whose house I have made the wilderness,
And the salt land his dwelling place.
He scorneth the tumult of the city,
Neither heareth he the shoutings of the driver.
The range of the mountains is his pasture,
And he searcheth after every green thing.
    Will the wild ox be content to serve thee?
Or will he abide by thy crib?
Canst thou bind the wild ox with his band in the furrow?
Or will he harrow the valleys after thee?
Wilt thou trust him, because his strength is great?
Or wilt thou leave to him thy labour?
Wilt thou confide in him, that he will bring home thy seed,
And gather the corn of thy threshing-floor?
    Hast thou given the horse his might?

Hast thou clothed his neck with the quivering mane?
Hast thou made him to leap as a locust?
The glory of his snorting is terrible.
He paweth in the valley, and rejoiceth in his strength:
He goeth out to meet the armed men.
He mocketh at fear, and is not dismayed;
Neither turneth he back from the sword.
The quiver rattleth against him,
The flashing spear and the javelin.
He swalloweth the ground with fierceness and rage;
Neither believeth he that it is the voice of the trumpet.
As oft as the trumpet soundeth he saith, "Aha!"
And he smelleth the battle afar off,
The thunder of the captains, and the shouting.
   Doth the hawk soar by thy wisdom,
And stretch her wings toward the south?
Doth the eagle mount up at thy command,
And make her nest on high?
She dwelleth on the rock, and hath her lodging there,
Upon the crag of the rock, and the strong hold
From thence she spieth out the prey;
Her eyes behold it afar off.
Her young ones also suck up blood:
And where the slain are, there is she.

Shall he that cavilleth contend with the Almighty?
He that argueth with God, let him answer it.
   Job. Behold, I am of small account; what shall I answer
     thee?
I lay my hand upon my mouth.
Once have I spoken, and I will not answer;
Yea twice, but I will proceed no further.
   Voice out of the Whirlwind. Gird up thy loins now
     like a man:
I will demand of thee, and declare thou unto me.
Wilt thou even disannul my judgment?
Wilt thou condemn me, that thou mayest be justified?
Or hast thou an arm like God?
And canst thou thunder with a voice like him?
Deck thyself now with excellency and dignity;
And array thyself with honour and majesty.

Pour forth the overflowings of thine anger:
And look upon every one that is proud, and abase him.
Look on every one that is proud, and bring him low;
And tread down the wicked where they stand.
Hide them in the dust together;
Bind their faces in the hidden place.
Then will I also confess of thee
That thine own right hand can save thee.

Job. I know that thou canst do all things,
And that no purpose of thine can be restrained.
"Who is this that hideth counsel without knowledge?"
Therefore have I uttered that which I understood not,
Things too wonderful for me, which I knew not.
Hear, I beseech thee, and I will speak;
I will demand of thee, and declare thou unto me.
I had heard of thee by the hearing of the ear;
But now mine eye seeth thee,
Wherefore I abhor myself, and repent
In dust and ashes.

Epilogue

And it was so, that after the Lord had spoken these words unto Job, the Lord said to Eliphaz the Temanite, "My wrath is kindled against thee, and against thy two friends: for ye have not spoken of me the thing that is right, as my servant Job hath. Now therefore, take unto you seven bullocks and seven rams, and go to my servant Job, and offer up for yourselves a burnt offering; and my servant Job shall pray for you; for him will I accept, that I deal not with you after your folly; for ye have not spoken of me the thing that is right, as my servant Job hath."

So Eliphaz the Temanite and Bildad the Shuhite and Zophar the Naamathite went, and did according as the Lord commanded them: and the Lord accepted Job.

And the Lord turned the captivity of Job, when he prayed for his friends: and the Lord gave Job twice as much as he had before. Then came there unto him all his brethren, and all his sisters, and all they that had been of his acquaintance before, and did eat bread with him in his house: and they bemoaned him, and comforted him concerning all the evil that the Lord had brought upon him: every man also gave him a piece of money, and every one a ring of gold.

So the Lord blessed the latter end of Job more than his beginning: and he had fourteen thousand sheep, and six thousand camels, and a thousand yoke of oxen, and a thousand she-asses. He had also seven sons and three daughters. And he called the name of the first, Jemimah; and the name of the second, Keziah; and the name of the third, Keren-happuch. And in all the land were no women found so fair as the daughters of Job: and their father gave them inheritance among their brethren. And after this Job lived a hundred and forty years, and saw his sons, and his sons' sons, even four generations. So Job died, being old and full of days.

ECCLESIASTES
Or, the Preacher

Introduction

THE words of the preacher, the son of David, king in Jerusalem.

Vanity of vanities,[1] saith the Preacher; vanity of vanities, all is vanity. What profit hath man of all his labour wherein he laboureth under the sun?

One generation goeth, and another generation cometh; and the earth abideth for ever. The sun also ariseth, and the sun goeth down, and hasteth to his place where he ariseth. The wind goeth toward the south, and turneth about unto the north; it turneth about continually in its course, and the wind returneth again to its circuits. All the rivers run into the sea, yet the sea is not full; unto the place whither the rivers go, thither they go again.

All things are full of weariness; man cannot utter it: the eye is not satisfied with seeing, nor the ear filled with hearing.

That which hath been is that which shall be; and that which hath been done is that which shall be done: and there is no new thing under the sun. Is there a thing whereof men say, "See, this is new"? It hath been already, in the ages which were before us.

There is no remembrance of the former generations; neither shall there be any remembrance of the latter generations that are to come, among those that shall come after.

[1] **vanity** the word meant *breath* or *vapor* and then *nothingness, vanity*

93

Essay I

I the Preacher was king over Israel in Jerusalem. And I applied my heart to seek and to search out by wisdom concerning all that is done under heaven: it is a sore travail that God hath given to the sons of men to be exercised therewith. I have seen all the works that are done under the sun; and, behold, all is vanity and a striving after wind. That which is crooked cannot be made straight: and that which is wanting cannot be numbered. I communed with mine own heart, saying, "Lo, I have gotten me great wisdom above all that were before me in Jerusalem: yea, my heart hath had great experience of wisdom and knowledge." And I applied my heart to know wisdom, and to know madness and folly: I perceived that this also was a striving after wind: For in much wisdom is much grief: and he that increaseth knowledge increaseth sorrow.

I said in mine heart, "Go to now, I will prove thee with mirth; therefore enjoy pleasure": and, behold, this also was vanity. I said of laughter, "It is mad": and of mirth, "What doeth it?" I searched in mine heart how to cheer my flesh with wine, mine heart yet guiding me with wisdom, and how to lay hold on folly, till I might see what it was good for the sons of men that they should do under the heaven all the days of their life. I made me great works; I builded me houses; I planted me vineyards; I made me gardens and parks, and I planted trees in them of all kinds of fruit: I made me pools of water, to water therefrom the forest where trees were reared. I bought menservants and maidens, and had servants born in my house; also I had great possessions of herds and flocks, above all that were before me in Jerusalem: I gathered me also silver and gold, and the peculiar treasure of kings and of the provinces. I got me men singers and women singers, and the delights of the sons of men, concubines very many. So I was great, and increased more than all that were before me in Jerusalem: also my wisdom remained with me. And whatsoever mine eyes desired I kept not from them: I withheld not my heart from any joy, for my heart rejoiced because of all

my labour; and this was my portion from all my labour.
Then I looked on all the works that my hands had wrought,
and on the labour that I had laboured to do: and, behold,
all was vanity and a striving after wind, and there was no
profit under the sun.

And I turned myself to behold wisdom, and madness and
folly: for what can the man do that cometh after the king?
even that which hath been already done. Then I saw that
wisdom excelleth folly, as far as light excelleth darkness.
The wise man's eyes are in his head, and the fool walketh
in darkness: and yet I perceived that one event happeneth
to them all. Then said I in my heart, "As it happeneth to
the fool, so will it happen even to me"; and why was I then
more wise? Then I said in my heart, that this also was
vanity. For of the wise man, even as of the fool, there is
no remembrance for ever; seeing that in the days to come
all will have been already forgotten. And how doth the wise
man die even as the fool! So I hated life; because the work
that is wrought under the sun was grievous unto me: for
all is vanity and a striving after wind.

And I hated all my labour wherein I laboured under the
sun: seeing that I must leave it unto the man that shall be
after me. And who knoweth whether he shall be a wise
man or a fool? yet shall he have rule over all my labour
wherein I have laboured, and wherein I have showed wisdom under the sun. This also is vanity. Therefore I turned
about to cause my heart to despair concerning all the labour
wherein I had laboured under the sun. For there is a man
whose labour is with wisdom, and with knowledge, and
with skilfulness; yet to a man that hath not laboured therein
shall he leave it for his portion. This also is vanity and a
great evil. For what hath a man of all his labour, and of the
striving of his heart, wherein he laboureth under the sun?
For all his days are but sorrows, and his travail is grief; yea,
even in the night his heart taketh no rest. This also is vanity.

There is nothing better for a man than that he should
eat and drink, and make his soul enjoy good in his labour.
This also I saw, that it is from the hand of God. For who
can eat, or who can have enjoyment, more than I? For to
the man that pleaseth him God giveth wisdom, and knowledge and joy: but to the sinner he giveth travail, to gather

and to heap up, that he may give to him that pleaseth God. This also is vanity and a striving after wind.

Essay II

To everything there is a season,
And a time to every purpose under the heaven:
A time to be born, and a time to die;
A time to plant, and a time to pluck up that which is
    planted;
A time to kill, and a time to heal;
A time to break down, and a time to build up;
A time to weep, and a time to laugh;
A time to mourn, and a time to dance;
A time to cast away stones, and a time to gather stones
    together;
A time to embrace, and a time to refrain from embracing;
A time to seek, and a time to lose;
A time to keep, and a time to cast away;
A time to rend, and a time to sew;
A time to keep silence, and a time to speak;
A time to love, and a time to hate;
A time for war, and a time for peace.

What profit hath he that worketh in that wherein he laboureth? I have seen the travail which God hath given to the sons of men to be exercised therewith. He hath made every thing beautiful in its time: also he hath set the world in their heart, yet so that man cannot find out the work that God hath done from the beginning even to the end.

I know that there is nothing better for them, than to rejoice, and to do good so long as they live. And also that every man should eat and drink, and enjoy good in all his labour, is the gift of God. I know that, whatsoever God doeth, it shall be for ever: nothing can be put to it, nor any thing taken from it: and God hath done it, that men should fear before him. That which is hath been already; and that which is to be hath already been: and God seeketh again that which is passed away.

And moreover I saw under the sun, in the place of judgment, that wickedness was there; and in the place of righteousness, that wickedness was there. I said in mine heart, "God shall judge the righteous and the wicked: for there is a time for every purpose and for every work." I said in mine heart, "It is because of the sons of men that God may prove them, and that they may see that they themselves are but as beasts." For that which befalleth the sons of men befalleth beasts; even one thing befalleth them: as the one dieth, so dieth the other; yea, they have all one breath; and man hath no pre-eminence above the beasts: for all is vanity. All go unto one place; all are of the dust, and all turn to dust again. Who knoweth the spirit of man whether it goeth upward, and the spirit of the beast whether it goeth downward to the earth? Wherefore I saw that there is nothing better, than that a man should rejoice in his works; for that is his portion: for who shall bring him back to see what shall be after him?

Then I returned and saw all the oppressions that are done under the sun: and behold, the tears of such as were oppressed, and they had no comforter; and on the side of their oppressors there was power, but they had no comforter. Wherefore I praised the dead which are already dead more than the living which are yet alive; yea, better than them both did I esteem him which hath not yet been, who hath not seen the evil work that is done under the sun.

Essay III

He that loveth silver shall not be satisfied with silver; nor he that loveth abundance with increase: this also is vanity. When goods increase, they are increased that eat them: and what advantage is there to the owner thereof, saving the beholding of them with his eyes? The sleep of a labouring man is sweet, whether he eat little or much: but the fulness of the rich will not suffer him to sleep.

There is a grievous evil which I have seen under the sun, namely, riches kept by the owner thereof to his hurt: and those riches perish by evil adventure; and if he hath begotten a son, there is nothing in his hand. As he came forth of his mother's womb, naked shall he go again as he came, and shall take nothing for his labour, which he may carry away in his hand. And this also is a grievous evil, that in all points as he came, so shall he go: and what profit hath he that he laboureth for the wind? All his days also he eateth in darkness, and he is sore vexed and hath sickness and wrath.

Behold, that which I have seen to be good and to be comely is for one to eat and to drink, and to enjoy good in all his labour, wherein he laboureth under the sun, all the days of his life which God hath given him: for this is his portion. Every man also to whom God hath given riches and wealth, and hath given him power to eat thereof, and to take his portion, and to rejoice in his labour; this is the gift of God. For he shall not much remember the days of his life; because God answereth him in the joy of his heart.

A good name is better than precious ointment; and the day of death than the day of one's birth. It is better to go to the house of mourning, than to go to the house of feasting: for that is the end of all men; and the living will lay it to his heart. Sorrow is better than laughter: for by the sadness of the countenance the heart is made glad. The heart of the wise is in the house of mourning; but the heart of fools is in the house of mirth. It is better to hear the rebuke of the wise, than for a man to hear the song of fools. For as the crackling of thorns under a pot, so is the laughter of the fool: this also is vanity.

Better is the end of a thing than the beginning thereof: and the patient in spirit is better than the proud in spirit. Be not hasty in thy spirit to be angry: for anger resteth in the bosom of fools. Say not thou, "What is the cause that the former days were better than these?" for thou dost not inquire wisely concerning this. Wisdom is as good as an inheritance: yea, more excellent is it for them that see the sun. For wisdom is a defence, even as money is a defence: but the excellency of knowledge is that wisdom preserveth the life of him that hath it. Consider the work of God: for who can make that straight, which he hath made crooked? In the day of prosperity be joyful, and in the day of adversity consider: God hath even made the one side by side with the other, to the end that man should not find out any thing that shall be after him.

All this have I seen in the days of my vanity: there is a righteous man that perisheth in his righteousness, and there is a wicked man that prolongeth his life in his evil-doing. Be not righteous over much; neither make thyself over wise: why shouldest thou destroy thyself? Be not over much wicked, neither be thou foolish: why shouldest thou die before thy time? It is good that thou shouldest take hold of this; yea, also from that withdraw not thine hand: for he that feareth God shall come forth of them all.

Essay IV

Wisdom is a strength to the wise man more than ten rulers which are in a city. Surely there is not a righteous man upon earth that doeth good, and sinneth not. Also take not heed unto all words that are spoken; lest thou hear thy servant curse thee: for oftentimes also thine own heart knoweth that thou thyself likewise hast cursed others.

There is a vanity which is done upon the earth; that there be righteous men, unto whom it happeneth according to the work of the wicked; again, there be wicked men, to whom it happeneth according to the work of the righteous: I said that this also is vanity. Then I commended mirth, because a man hath no better thing under the sun than to eat, and to drink, and to be merry: for that shall abide with him in his labour all the days of his life which God hath given him under the sun.

When I applied my heart to know wisdom, and to see the business that is done upon the earth (for also there is that neither day nor night seeth sleep with his eyes): then I beheld all the work of God, that man cannot find out the work that is done under the sun: because however much a man labour to seek it out, yet he shall not find it; yea moreover, though a wise man think to know it, yet shall he not be able to find it.

For all this I laid to my heart, even to explore all this; that the righteous, and the wise, and their works, are in the hand of God: whether it be love or hatred, man knoweth it not; all is before them. All things come alike to all: there is one event to the righteous and to the wicked; to the good and to the clean and to the unclean; to him that sacrificeth and to him that sacrificeth not: as is the good, so is the sinner; and he that sweareth, as he that feareth an oath. This is an evil in all that is done under the sun, that there is one event unto all: yea also, the heart of the sons of men is full of evil, and madness is in their heart while they live, and after that they go to the dead. For to him that is joined with all the living there is hope: for a living dog is better than a dead lion. For the living know that they shall die: but the dead know not any thing, neither have they any more a reward; for the memory of them is forgotten. As well their love, as their hatred and their envy, is now perished; neither have they any more a portion for ever in any thing that is done under the sun.

Go thy way, eat thy bread with joy, and drink thy wine with a merry heart; for God hath already accepted thy works. Let thy garments be always white; and let not thy head lack ointment. Live joyfully with the wife whom thou lovest all the days of the life of thy vanity, which he hath given thee under the sun, all the days of thy vanity: for that is thy portion in life, and in thy labour wherein thou labourest under the sun. Whatsoever thy hand findeth to do, do it with thy might; for there is no work, nor device, nor knowledge, nor wisdom, in the grave, whither thou goest.

I returned, and saw under the sun that the race is not to the swift, nor the battle to the strong, neither yet bread to the wise, nor yet riches to men of understanding, nor yet favour to men of skill; but time and chance happeneth to them all. For man also knoweth not his time: as the fishes that are taken in an evil net, and as the birds that are caught in the snare, even so are the sons of men snared in an evil time, when it falleth suddenly upon them.

Cast thy bread upon the waters:
For thou shalt find it after many days.

Give a portion to seven, yea, even unto eight;
For thou knowest not what evil shall be upon the earth.

If the clouds be full of rain,
They empty themselves upon the earth:
And if a tree fall toward the south, or toward the north,
In the place where the tree falleth, there shall it be.

He that observeth the wind shall not sow;
And he that regardeth the clouds shall not reap.

As thou knowest not what is the way of the wind,
Nor how the bones do grow in the womb of her that is with
    child;
Even so thou knowest not the work of God who doeth all.
In the morning sow thy seed,
And in the evening withhold not thine hand:
For thou knowest not which shall prosper,
Whether this or that, or whether they both shall be alike
    good.

Essay V

Truly the light is sweet, and a pleasant thing it is for the eyes to behold the sun. Yea, if a man live many years, let him rejoice in them all; but let him remember the days of darkness, for they shall be many. All that cometh is vanity.

Rejoice, O young man, in thy youth; and let thy heart cheer thee in the days of thy youth, and walk in the ways of thine heart, and in the sight of thine eyes: but know thou, that for all these things God will bring thee into judgment. Therefore remove sorrow from thy heart, and put away evil from thy flesh: for youth and the prime of life are vanity.

Remember also thy Creator in the days of thy youth,
Or ever the evil days come,
And the years draw nigh, when thou shalt say,
"I have no pleasure in them";
Or ever the sun, and the light,
And the moon, and the stars, be darkened,

And the clouds return after the rain:
In the day when the keepers of the house shall tremble,
And the strong men shall bow themselves,
And the grinders cease because they are few,
And those that look out of the windows be darkened,
And the doors shall be shut in the street;
When the sound of the grinding is low,
And one shall rise up at the voice of a bird,
And all the daughters of music shall be brought low;
Yea, they shall be afraid of that which is high,
And terrors shall be in the way;
And the almond tree shall blossom,
And the grasshopper shall be a burden,
And the caper-berry shall fail:
Because man goeth to his long home,
And the mourners go about the streets:
Or ever the silver cord be loosed,
Or the golden bowl be broken,
Or the pitcher be broken at the fountain,
Or the wheel broken at the cistern;
And the dust return to the earth as it was,
And the spirit return unto God who gave it.

Vanity of vanities, saith the Preacher; all is vanity.

And further, because the Preacher was wise, he still taught the people knowledge; yea, he pondered, and sought out, and set in order many proverbs. The Preacher sought to find out acceptable words, and that which was written uprightly, even words of truth.

The words of the wise are as goads, and as nails well fastened are the words of the masters of assemblies, which are given from one shepherd. And furthermore, my son, be admonished: of making many books there is no end; and much study is a weariness of the flesh.

This is the end of the matter; all hath been heard: fear God, and keep his commandments; for this is the whole duty of man. For God shall bring every work into judgment, with every hidden thing, whether it be good or whether it be evil.

THE SONG OF SONGS[1]

I

THE BRIDE

Let him kiss me with the kisses of his mouth:
For thy love is better than wine.
Thine ointments have a goodly fragrance;
Thy name is an ointment poured forth;
Therefore do the virgins love thee.

THE CHORUS

Draw me. We will run after thee.

THE BRIDE

The king hath brought me into his chambers.

THE CHORUS

We will be glad and rejoice in thee,
We will make mention of thy love more than of wine:
Rightly do they love thee.

THE BRIDE

I am black, but comely,
O ye daughters of Jerusalem,

[1] The ascription of speeches to bride, bridegroom, etc. in this volume adapts the arrangements of Richard Moulton (*The Modern Readers Bible*, Macmillan) and of Ernest Sutherland Bates (*The Bible Designed to be Read as Living Literature*, Simon and Schuster)

As the tents of Kedar,
As the curtains of Solomon.
Look not upon me, because I am swarthy,
Because the sun hath scorched me.

My mother's sons were incensed against me,
They made me keeper of the vineyards;
But mine own vineyard have I not kept.

Tell me, O thou whom my soul loveth,
Where thou feedest thy flock, where thou makest it to rest
    at noon:
For why should I be as one that is veiled
Beside the flocks of thy companions?

THE BRIDEGROOM

If thou know not, O thou fairest among women,
Go thy way forth by the footsteps of the flock,
And feed thy kids beside the shepherds' tents.

I have compared thee, O my love,
To a steed in Pharaoh's chariots.
Thy cheeks are comely with plaits of hair,
Thy neck with strings of jewels.
We will make thee plaits of gold
With studs of silver.

THE BRIDE

While the king sat at his table,
My spikenard sent forth its fragrance.
My beloved is unto me as a bundle of myrrh,
That lieth betwixt my breasts.
My beloved is unto me as a cluster of henna-flowers
In the vineyards of En-gedi.

THE BRIDEGROOM

Behold, thou art fair, my love; behold, thou art fair;
Thine eyes are as doves.

THE BRIDE

Behold, thou art fair, my beloved, yea, pleasant:
Also our couch is green.
The beams of our house are cedars,
And our rafters are firs.

I am a rose of Sharon,
A lily of the valleys.

THE BRIDEGROOM

As a lily among thorns,
So is my love among the daughters.

THE BRIDE

As the apple tree among the trees of the wood,
So is my beloved among the sons.
I sat down under his shadow with great delight,
And his fruit was sweet to my taste.

He brought me to the banqueting house,
And his banner over me was love.
Stay ye me with raisins, comfort me with apples:
For I am sick of love.[2]
His left hand is under my head,
And his right hand doth embrace me.

I adjure you, O daughters of Jerusalem,
By the roes, and by the hinds of the field,
That ye stir not up, nor awaken love,
Until it please.

[2] **sick of love** lovesick

II

THE BRIDE

The voice of my beloved! behold, he cometh,
Leaping upon the mountains, skipping upon the hills.
My beloved is like a roe or a young hart:
Behold, he standeth behind our wall,
He looketh in at the windows,
He showeth himself through the lattice.
My beloved spoke, and said unto me,
"Rise up, my love, my fair one, and come away.
For, lo, the winter is past,
The rain is over and gone;
The flowers appear on the earth;
The time of the singing of birds is come,
And the voice of the turtle [3] is heard in our land;
The fig tree ripeneth her green figs,
And the vines are in blossom,
They give forth their fragrance.
Arise, my love, my fair one, and come away.
O my dove, that art in the clefts of the rock, in the covert
    of the steep place,
Let me see thy countenance, let me hear thy voice;
For sweet is thy voice, and thy countenance is comely."

THE BROTHERS

Take us the foxes, the little foxes, that spoil the vineyard;
For our vineyards are in blossom.

THE BRIDE

My beloved is mine, and I am his:
He feedeth his flock among the lilies.
Until the day be cool, and the shadows flee away,

[3] **turtle** turtle dove

Turn, my beloved, and be thou like a roe or a young hart
Upon the mountains of Bether.
By night on my bed I sought him whom my soul loveth:
I sought him, but I found him not.
I said, "I will rise now, and go about the city,
In the streets and in the broad ways,
I will seek him whom my soul loveth":
I sought him, but I found him not.
The watchmen that go about the city found me:
To whom I said, "Saw ye him whom my soul loveth?"
It was but a little that I passed from them,
When I found him whom my soul loveth:
I held him, and would not let him go,
Until I had brought him into my mother's house,
And into the chamber of her that conceived me.

I adjure you, O daughters of Jerusalem,
By the roes, and by the hinds of the field,
That ye stir not up, nor awaken love,
Until it please.

III

THE BRIDEGROOM

Behold thou art fair, my love; behold, thou art fair;
Thine eyes are as doves behind thy veil:
Thy hair is as a flock of goats,
That lie along the side of Mount Gilead.

Thy teeth are like a flock of ewes that are newly shorn,
Which are come up from the washing;
Whereof every one hath twins,
And none is bereaved among them.

Thy lips are like a thread of scarlet,
And thy mouth is comely:
Thy temples are like a piece of pomegranate
Behind thy veil.

Thy neck is like the tower of David builded for an armoury,
Whereon there hang a thousand bucklers,
All the shields of the mighty men.
Thy two breasts are like two fawns that are twins of a roe,
Which feed among the lilies.
Until the day be cool, and the shadows flee away,
I will get me to the mountain of myrrh,
And to the hill of frankincense.

Thou hast ravished my heart, my sister, my bride;
Thou hast ravished my heart with one of thine eyes.
With one chain of thy neck.
How fair is thy love, my sister, my bride!
How much better is thy love than wine!
And the smell of thine ointments than all manner of spices!
Thy lips, O my bride, drop as the honeycomb:
Honey and milk are under thy tongue;
And the smell of thy garments is like the smell of Lebanon.

IV

THE BRIDE

I was asleep, but my heart waked:
It is the voice of my beloved that knocketh, saying,
"Open to me, my sister, my love, my dove, my undefiled:
For my head is filled with dew,
My locks with the drops of the night."

I have put off my coat; how shall I put it on?
I have washed my feet; how shall I defile them?
My beloved put in his hand by the hole of the door,
And my heart was moved for him.
I rose up to open to my beloved;
And my hands dropped with myrrh,
And my fingers with liquid myrrh,
Upon the handles of the bolt.

I opened to my beloved;
But my beloved had withdrawn himself, and was gone.

My soul had failed me when he spoke:
I sought him, but I could not find him;
I called him, but he gave me no answer.
The watchmen that go about the city found me,
They smote me, they wounded me;
The keepers of the walls took away my mantle from me.

I adjure you, O daughters of Jerusalem, if ye find my be-
    loved,
That ye tell him, that I am sick of love.

THE CHORUS

What is thy beloved more than another beloved,
O thou fairest among women?
What is thy beloved more than another beloved,
That thou dost so adjure us?

THE BRIDE

My beloved is white and ruddy,
The chiefest among ten thousand.
His head is as the most fine gold,
His locks are bushy, and black as a raven.
His eyes are like doves beside the water brooks;
Washed with milk, and fitly set.
His cheeks are as a bed of spices, as banks of sweet herbs:

His lips are as lilies, dropping liquid myrrh.
His hands are as rings of gold set with beryl:
His body is as ivory work overlaid with sapphires.
His legs are as pillars of marble, set upon sockets of fine
    gold:
His aspect is like Lebanon, excellent as the cedars.
His mouth is most sweet: yea, he is altogether lovely.
This is my beloved, and this is my friend,
O daughters of Jerusalem.

V

THE BRIDEGROOM

How beautiful are thy feet in sandals, O prince's daughter!
The joints of thy thighs are like jewels,
The work of the hands of a cunning workman.

Thy navel is like a round goblet,
Wherein no mingled wine is wanting:
Thy belly is like a heap of wheat
Set about with lilies.

Thy two breasts are like two fawns
That are twins of a roe.
Thy neck is like the tower of ivory;
Thine eyes as the pools in Heshbon, by the gate of Bath-
    rabbim;
Thy nose is like the tower of Lebanon
Which looketh toward Damascus.

Thine head upon thee is like Carmel,
And the hair of thine head like purple;
The king is held captive in the tresses thereof.
How fair and how pleasant art thou,
O love, for delights!
This thy stature is like to a palm tree,
And thy breasts to clusters of grapes.

I said, "I will climb up into the palm tree,
I will take hold of the branches thereof":
Let thy breasts be as clusters of the vine,
And the smell of thy breath like apples;
And thy mouth like the best wine,
That goeth down smoothly for my beloved,
Gliding through the lips of those that are asleep.

THE BRIDE

I am my beloved's,
And his desire is toward me.
Come, my beloved, let us go forth into the field;
Let us lodge in the villages.

Let us get up early to the vineyards;
Let us see whether the vine hath budded, and its blossom
be open,
And the pomegranates be in flower:

There will I give thee my love.
The mandrakes give forth fragrance,
And at our doors are all manner of precious fruits, new
and old.
Which I have laid up for thee, O my beloved.

VI

THE CHORUS

Who is this that cometh up from the wilderness,
Leaning upon her beloved?

THE BRIDE

Set me as a seal upon thine heart, as a seal upon thine arm:
For love is strong as death;
Jealousy is cruel as the grave:
The flashes thereof are flashes of fire,
A very flame of the Lord.
Many waters cannot quench love,
Neither can the floods drown it:
If a man would give all the substance of his house for love,
He would utterly be contemned.

THE BRIDEGROOM

Thou that dwellest in the gardens,
The companions hearken for thy voice:
Cause me to hear it.

THE BRIDE

Make haste, my beloved,
And be thou like to a roe or to a young hart
Upon the mountains of spices.

Bibliography

REFERENCE WORKS

The Abingdon Bible Commentary, ed. Frederick C. Eiseler and Edwin Lewis, Abingdon, 1929.

M. S. Miller and J. Lane Miller, *Harper's Bible Dictionary*, Harper, 1959.

Encyclopedia Biblica, ed. Thos. K. Cheyne, 4 vols., London, 1914.

The Interpreter's Bible, 12 vols., Abingdon Press, 1956. Essays and articles by various Biblical specialists.

GENERAL

G. A. Bewer, *The Literature of the Old Testament*, rev. ed., Columbia Press, 1933.

Mary Ellen Chase, *The Bible for the Common Reader*, New York, 1945.

Frederick Kenyon, *The Story of the Bible: A Popular Account of How It Came to Be*, New York, 1937. From early manuscripts to English translations.

Bernard W. Anderson, *Understanding the Old Testament*, Prentice-Hall, 1957. An analysis of the O.T. in its historical context and an evaluation of its contribution.

Harry M. Orlinsky, *Ancient Israel*, Cornell U. Press, 1958. An excellent brief history of O.T. times.

Martin Noth, *The History of Israel*, Harper, 1958.

G. Earnest Wright, *Biblical Archaeology*, Westminster Press, 1957. Illustrated.

J. Philip Hyatt, *Prophetic Religion*, Abingdon, 1947. Short studies of seven prophets, including five represented in this text.

J. M. P. Powis Smith, *The Prophets and their Times*, Chicago Press, rev. 1941.

SPECIAL STUDIES

Wisdom Literature: *Anderson* (op. cit.) chap. 15; *Bewer* (op. cit.) chap. 15; "Wisdom Literature," *Interpreter's Bible,* vol. I, pp. 212-219.

Job: Samuel T. Terrien, *Interpreter's Bible,* vol. III; *Bewer* (op. cit.) pp. 316-330; Samuel Sandmel, *The Hebrew Scriptures,* Knopf, 1963, chap. 22.

Psalms, Song of Songs: *Sandmel* (op. cit.) chap. 24; *Bewer* (op. cit.) chap. 20; Robert Gordis, *The Song of Songs,* Jewish Theological Seminary, 1954.